THE DAY SHE LEFT

Survivor's Diary

Stories of Transforming Trauma Into Triumph

VOL. 2

Visionary Author
Tamara C. Gooch

Table of Contents

Introduction 1

The Butterfly Emerges – Darline Chudoba. 5

Priceless Moments of God's Faithfulness – Tamara A. Baldwin. . .15

Free Indeed – Pamela Nance Johnson. 35

From Broken Pieces to Peace – Mona Griffin 49

Childhood Nightmare – Victoria Serratos 63

Better not Bitter – Anedra R. Eatman 79

About The Visionary Author 89

Introduction

Fear not, for I am with you; be not dismayed, for I am your God; I will strengthen you, I will help you, I will uphold you with my righteous right hand. – Isaiah 41:10, NIV

Trauma can stem from an early childhood ordeal, a divorce, intimate partner violence, abuse or even bullying. It could result in nightmares, sleepless nights, feeling jumpy, stress, flashbacks or feeling overwhelmed. Over half of Americans will go through at least one traumatic event in their lives. Trauma that causes stress to our mind and body can affect us in physical ways such as headaches, upset stomach, muscle tension and fatigue. What does trauma look like for you?

When things such as this take place oftentimes the dark cloud of depression consumes most, and the course of action is to shrink away or become angry. Then you have those who choose a different route and decide to pour that anger and depression out on paper by journal/diary. The therapy that can come from pouring your heart out on paper allows you to stop holding on to that very thing that caused so much internal trauma.

We open our diaries and give you a sneak peek into *The Day She Left, Survivor's Diary: Stories of Transforming Trauma into Triumph, Volume 2.* This powerful compilation shares stories of women showing how they were able to overcome traumas and begin the transformation to a triumphant life. Join us on this quest.

You may be that woman who has diary upon diary of stories you have emptied out from your heart to see your way forward with a genuine smile. If that is you, we invite you to take this journey with us to freedom. We invite you to share in our triumphant victories and embody the true essence of living authentically with no guilt, shame, or embarrassment.

Tamara C. Gooch – Visionary Author

THE DAY SHE LEFT

Survivor's Diary

VOL. 2

Darline Cherisme Chudoba is a Renaissance Goals Coach. Throughout her life she had much pain and suffering. The hardest thing she had to endure was life after an abusive marriage. She thought life was over for her and her three children when they left for good. There were many days she was depressed and wanted to end her life, however there was still a little bit of hope inside of her, especially when she looked at her children.

Darline is now living independently with her three children. She is financially stable and running multiple businesses. She has embraced being a Renaissance Goals Coach as well as a Renaissance Freelance Teacher. She works mainly with survivors of trauma, and/or abuse so they can accept their past, connect with others, and transform their lives. That's what her company, A.C.T Consultants stands for. She empowers people to crush their goals.

Darlene Chudoba

The Butterfly Emerges

Darline Chudoba

The way we met; you would think that our relationship would actually end up being a great one. I mean, we met at church. It was like a romantic movie. Here I was, 24 years old and I had never had a real relationship before. I was living on my own for the first time in the town where I graduated college several months prior. At that time, it truly did not look weird to me that whenever there was an event or a program at the church, he was either walking in minutes after I arrived, or he would already be there before I arrived. No, I did not find it weird at all. On two occasions he asked me to join him for brunch with several of his other friends from church. However, at those times, I was on the schedule to work after church. On the third Sunday, he came boldly to me to ask me once again and this time I said yes because I happened to be off. I will not lie, I had a great time connecting with him and the others and started to form strong friendships with those people, which have continued till today.

I used to think about what would have happened if I did not say yes on the third attempt, but I soon realized that you cannot live in the shoulda-coulda life sentence. It is what it is. Indeed, I found out that he had planned on asking me one more time to join him and his friends for the brunch; if I had said no for the third time then he would have let it go. Innocent, right? Wrong! This man knew that it was my first time living on my own. He knew that my Haitian parents did not approve of me doing so because they had their own plans for me after I graduated college. He knew that I craved approval, acceptance and love. You know how he knew? Because I talked about it with him and a few others that I grew close to from the church.

I ended up being able to change jobs and did not work on Sundays any longer. So, the Sunday brunches continued with the group. I saw him as a good friend. I learned some things about him over the subsequent months. During the Christmas holiday, he ended up getting a job in North Carolina. He had to move there by the New Year. He and the youth pastor who I grew close to asked me to come over for Christmas dinner. I was happy to say yes because I was not going to visit my family for the holidays. Therefore, I spent Christmas with him, the youth pastor, his wife, and their family. I saw that he was not the same as a few weeks before and I saw a sadness in his eyes during the dinner, but I did not put two and two together.

Anyway, he went ahead and moved. However, we kept in contact through email. One day, I received an email from him saying that he missed seeing my smile and wished I were there with him. So, I sent him an email asking him jokingly if he was flirting with me. He replied that he would like my work number because he had to talk to me; it was important. Within 20 minutes he called me while I was at my desk at work. He told me that he really liked me, and he really cared for me. He said that he would come to the different events at the church hoping that I was there or that I was on my way. He would ask different people there if they had seen me. He explained that he wanted to ask me to date him; however, he was not sure if I wanted to have a long-distance relationship.

That phone call changed the course and direction of my life. That's how it all began, so innocently and so sweetly. Our relationship moved fast: One minute we were good friends; the next minute I was on a plane going to North Carolina to spend a week with him; and within 4 months, I left my life in New Jersey and moved in with him in North Carolina.

The abuse started within weeks of me moving to North Carolina. It started with him verbally abusing me. I was too ashamed and felt guilty about leaving my life in New Jersey to start a life with him in North Carolina. The person that I was back then was not strong enough to live up to people saying "I told you so," because many people did not agree with me moving there to be with him in the first place. The abuse became physical, mental, and financial in less than six months. In North Carolina I only knew him for the most part. I did try to become friends with those I worked with to see about getting a place to share so that I would not be with this man anymore. Unfortunately, I had no one to move into an apartment with; therefore, I continued to stay with him. He proposed to me a few months later and I ended up saying yes. The red flags did not deter me from saying yes because like I said, I felt like I had to continue because I did not want to hear "I told you so." I felt that I could make it work if I prayed enough; if I spoke to him and if I tried my best to do good then the abuse wouldn't happen. We got married five months later. Two months afterward, I got pregnant with our first son. Then, over a year later, I got pregnant with our daughter, then a few months after I gave birth to our daughter, I got pregnant with our last child.

My oldest was born in North Carolina, but when he was almost one year old, we moved back to New Jersey because my husband's job did not work out after all. I had become a stay-at-home mom basically overnight by caring for our firstborn. There is one incident that sticks in my mind. I did some research about abuse and anger management. Through my search to make our marriage better, I found out that there was help out there for those who truly wanted to change. During that time, he hadn't physically abused me yet, meaning he had not put his hands on me. He would, however, corner me and call me a bitch and other names; he would scream and spit in my face while he said if I didn't want to be part of the team I could leave, but without my children. He would literally have me shaking in my boots because he was taller and weighed about 200 pounds. I was only about 110 pounds.

I went to him after doing the research and said calmly that he needed to get some anger management classes. I said for this marriage to be better, he needed to get some help. He screamed and yelled words such as f*** you over six times. He claimed that there was nothing wrong with him. He didn't need any help and I could get the hell out of his life because he didn't need me nor my offer of him getting help. He claimed that what would actually help is if I did do what he told me to do the first time. He came to me in the kitchen. There was something in his eyes that I had never seen before, pure rage. He grabbed my arm and twisted it behind my back. He then dragged me outside without a coat or shoes on me in the middle of winter. He shoved me and closed the door and locked me out of the house. Meanwhile, my kids were screaming and crying for me by the glass door. All I could do was kneel on the ground and pray, and I kept telling the kids that everything would be okay. After about 10 minutes, he opened the door and pulled me back inside.

Later in the week, he decided to tell his mother what happened, but of course he blamed me, saying that I told him he needed help and that he was a terrible person. His mother got so angry that she called the police to escort me and my children out of her house. Yes, at this point, we were living in one of her houses. I called my mom and youngest brother and they came. When the police arrived, my husband went ahead and told them about the incident that took place only days before. Now I do not know why he told them this; I don't know if it was out of guilt or what. One of the police officers came to me and asked if I wanted to file a report against him for physical abuse. I was scared because I did not know what would happen to me and the kids. With my brother's encouragement, I did file a report. He was put in jail and I got a restraining order against him. This was all because I tried to get him some help, telling him if we wanted the marriage to work out, he had to get some anger management and that what he had been doing, verbally abusing me, calling me the B word and screaming at me and spitting while he was speaking to me, cornering me because he was taller and bigger than me—all that did was create fear in me. He made me feel like a trapped animal, like I couldn't do anything. That would be the first restraining order of many that I got and dropped because he made me believe that things would be different.

For six years, I remained a stay-at-home mom raising our three children; therefore, I did not have my own money. I didn't have a job so leaving him would be difficult. I did try to leave him several times. However due to not being financially stable, I came back. It seems to me looking back now that going back to him truly made the abuse a lot worse each time, especially the verbal and mental abuse. I felt like I had no other choice but to be with this man. He would tell me that I couldn't make it without him, and I believed him. The moment that changed the outcome of my life was when my oldest ended up getting abused by him verbally for just being a kid, then within that day my oldest ended up acting out with abuse toward me. I remember getting him ready to go outside to play because I felt he stayed in the house for too long watching different shows; he ended up slapping me—not hard, but he ended up slapping me in the face and that, coupled with him getting abused by his father, really opened my eyes to wanting to leave, and this time, to leave for good.

Now I did not plan on leaving when I did; however, it just all played out well for me to leave. I ended up developing a really bad mental illness because of all the trauma and the abuse that I suffered in those last six years of being with my now ex-husband. I ended up in the hospital off and on until 2019. I would have manic episodes and depression periods. It has been a challenge for me to get up in the morning every day to take care of my children and to take care of myself. There were times when I thought about committing suicide and there were times when I wanted to just get in my car and drive away. It was such a difficult time for me raising my children by myself, having to provide for their needs and wants, and dealing with my mental illness. The journey, although it was challenging, has truly been rewarding, to say the least. I have not seen the inside of a mental ward hospital since 2019 and I plan on making sure that I never see one again. I have been working hard and keeping myself together so that I do not have another manic episode.

Back in 2015, life started to truly take a change for the better. I was invited to a women's empowerment conference. That ended up being one of the most important turn-arounds in my life. The conference was organized by a good friend of mine that I grew up with in my childhood church. After the conference, that evening birthed Accept.Connect.Transform A.C.T. Consultants. Within the week after the conference, I registered the business. I did not do too much with the business throughout the next few years; however, whenever ideas came in my mind, I wrote them down and just kept a diary of what I wanted to do. I birthed my "Discover Yourself & Your Purpose Program" and the "Keep Goaling" motto and program. Some years later, I was able to start a women's group underneath the business, A.C.T Consultants. I helped these women who were either homeless and/or struggling with their own trauma and abuse to focus on themselves, their goals, and their dreams so that they could begin to live a better life. We met every week for about nine months. I even had other successful women come in to speak to the women about various topics that would help them to get to a better place in their lives. I was able to do the work about a year after 2015 and so the methods, the exercise, the things I learned and the things I put together were what I used to work with these women.

I believe that whatever trauma, whatever abuse a person goes through, it is not for that person; it is for those who need it most so that they can learn from your story and not have the same experience or to get the strength they need to get out of the situation. After dealing with the trauma and the abuse with my ex-husband, I can truly say in 2021 that I am grateful that I did go through it because it has made me the person that I am today. It has given me the strength I need to be able to fight anything that comes my way, to be strong enough and help others to do the same.

My trauma has become a triumph for me and my children. I am now a Renaissance Goals Coach, Freelance Teacher, and content writer. As a Renaissance Goals Coach, I help women who are survivors of trauma and/or abuse to focus on themselves, their goals, and their dreams so that they can have a better, more fulfilling life.

I coach these women in one-on-one sessions or group programs to accept their scars, do the work and emerge to be beautiful butterflies. I help them to accept their past and connect them with others so that their lives can be transformed. As a freelance teacher I am happy to be able to teach ages three to adulthood various subjects, for example, cooking, Haitian Creole, self-esteem, black history, social, sewing, and fashion design. As a content writer I have been helping others to create a better social media image for their clients and customers.

I love myself so much more within the last few years. I know that I am enough. I know that I can do all things if I believe in it and put the work in it. I have been helping women for over eight years now; even when I was dealing with my mess, I was able to help others to get to a better point in their lives. When I look back at where I was and where I am now, I am in so much awe at the goodness and gracious mercy of God. My children and I have been living in our own nice apartment where we all have our own rooms, and I even have an office where I conduct my businesses. I have peace in my heart because I have let go of my part in my traumatic experiences, because I am a different person today than I was back then. I have forgiven myself for deciding to stay in a relationship with someone who abused me so much. I have even forgiven my ex-husband for all he did to me. I have developed a great presence on social media as I daily help women to stay motivated and strong as they navigate their lives after their trauma and/or abuse. I am teaching them through videos and going live to want to live a life of purpose. I am teaching them that they are loved, even with their scars. I am helping them to understand that they are enough and that right now they need to be like a caterpillar who is going into a cocoon. During the cocoon process, with my help and guidance, they will be able to emerge like a beautiful butterfly. I let them know that they are not alone and that although the work and process may be difficult, if I could do the work, they can, too. My videos are there to teach them about not only being strong in their life right now, but I give them hope that their past is truly not a life sentence, but a lesson that they have to learn and grow from. This is what I learned about my life and I am passing this knowledge to others. I am thankful for the scars. I am thankful for the traumas because I am now equipped to help others deal with various types of abuse and trauma.

Toastmaster's International award-winning public speaker, Reverend Tamara Baldwin is a highly motivated, mother, educator, philanthropist, family advocate, job readiness/career counselor and academic advocate for underserved populations. To include, alternative education, special-needs, adult education, first generation graduates, and juvenile offenders, within the South Carolina department of corrections. Tamara is the founder of Priceless Moments Consulting where she demonstrates her life purpose of encouraging, empowering, and equipping those whom she encounters to live with intentionality.

Tamara holds a Ministry Leadership Master's Degree from Grand Rapids Theological Seminary in Grand Rapids, Michigan, and will complete her second master's degree toward licensure as a Professional Counselor in the spring of 2022. Tamara is a native of Ann Arbor, Michigan, residing in Grand Rapids, Michigan, before relocating to South Carolina. Tamara desires to live an examined life in order that God will be glorified. "It is my desire to live an examined life that pleases God, and to sow by serving others as God's hand extended."

Priceless Moments of God's Faithfulness

Tamara A. Baldwin

I am not the first to experience being hurt, abused, misunderstood, misrepresented, overlooked, judged, marginalized, taken for granted. Nor will I be the last. However, I have by God's saving grace learned his grace is sufficient and his mercies never cease. Our identity in Christ is the foundation of every challenge we face. Therefore, as we encounter physical, mental, emotional, spiritual and financial challenges we must note that we are also living in a time where people proclaim Christ, yet do not live Christ. We speak faith, yet live fear. We declare, yet really live in defeat. We claim to be speaking our truth, yet we are really trampling on those who have endured with us. Moreover, to suggest by declaration this is "just who I am" begs the question who are you through God's eyes? Yes, the older saints and ain'ts had a compelling point. When you know better you do better. This is only accurate as long as we recognize where we are and where we are not as it relates to our identity in Christ. God's word says, "I will guide you along the best pathway for your life. I will advise you and watch over you." Psalm 32:8, NLT

God specifically and explicitly assures us that we are never alone. We don't have to guess, wonder, surmise, or search. He has been, is and always will be. I am reminded of moments along the journey where because of my upbringing I continuously love, give, forgive, adjust, sacrifice, compromise, pivot, and shift. In fact, it is this lifelong manner of working for which I am known. I am a friend who since I can remember has always been trustworthy, honest, non-judgmental, and accommodating, typically leaving an encounter depleted rather than fueled. Indeed, I have been jolted into a reality that I am more of a friend to individuals I perceived as friends, but who rather seek/sought to use me for what I freely share. My nature is not to perceive being used as much as it is feeling honored to be thought of to meet a need. God's faithfulness allows me to see this as a priceless moment of serving as His hand extended in the world.

Furthermore, I believe our upbringing is directly linked to who we are. Surprisingly, and in contrast, the necessity and need to care for others was the result of experiencing the opposite. Growing up in an affluent home and multicultural neighborhood there was an expectation to stand tall, with head up, shoulders back, precise diction ensuring every syllable was used as per vocabulary and dictionary specifications. Eye contact and a firm handshake, only in the event the individuals I would greet were acceptable in their self-presentation.

Indeed, living under a spotlight or in a fishbowl of sorts was also a rarity for one of six black families in Ann Arbor. It was then that I developed the first of many layers of protection from the beginning of what has grown into a lifetime of being viewed but not regarded. Reflecting on my childhood home and neighborhood just blocks from the University of Michigan Football Stadium, (also known as "The Big House"), I vividly recall my parents ensuring that my siblings and I were exposed to what would now be classified as diversity and inclusion.

Interaction with neighbors of different backgrounds was cele-brated rather than tolerated. Whether meals were at the home of someone else or our own home, they were always different. My parents were masterminds with their decision to be intentional relating to their understanding of how important it was to expose their children to diverse populations. My mother and father may or may not have known that what they did and were doing would shape my cultural identity and socialization.

For instance, my cultural identity is that of an American Indian, African American, Non-Hispanic Latino, Heterosexual Sexual, Upper Middle Class, Christian, Female with a Master's Degree in Ministry Leadership; the above identities intersect in ways that are surprisingly noble and at times ashamedly naive in perception. I grew up in an upper class two-parent family. My father was sole provider, working as an educator, psychoanalyst and Assistant Superintendent of schools as well as Director of Curriculum and State/Federal programming. In our home there was a spoken and unspoken expectation that academic achievement was a key value for someone born into the Baldwin family.

I am the eldest child of four, fraternal twin girls, and two single birth boys. We were raised to be proud, while being instructed: "stand up straight," don't mumble—speak up," "hold your head up high," "pos-ture, posture, pay attention to your posture." This privileged identity was woven into the fabric of everything we did, everywhere we went, including those with whom we were permitted to associate. A true alpha male, my father ensured that my mother was well taken care of. Mother was a domestic engineer who ensured meals were prepared and the house meticulously tidy before Father arrived home from one of his various jobs. Upon his arrival home Mother made sure we were neat clean and ready to greet Father as he entered the house.

In our home remembering who we were and where we came from was paramount and included the following statements: "You need to work twice as hard." "You are just as smart as anyone in your school." "You are a Baldwin." "What goes on in this house stays in this house." "When you get to school you better listen and learn." "Do not embarrass me." "Your grandparents are expecting great things from you." "There are people who died trying to get what you have." "You better appreciate what you have and where you live." From these assertions, daily instructions and systems of belief, my cultural identity was shaped. My parents were on what I believe to be a united mission to create a foundation for which I am grateful. My privileged upbringing at home, school, church and in the community is where I saw my parents' model, demonstrate, and facilitate our proper cultural identity, racial history, and heritage as an educated, affluent African American family.

Now as an adult I am aware that while my experiences are real, faint echoes remain of comments such as "You think you're better than just because your family has money." Another echo is "You all just some 'uppity Negros.'" Similarly, regarding my socialization, our family was one of only six black families in the Ann Arbor, Michigan neighborhood where I grew up. My cultural identity was welcomed, embraced, shared and celebrated. Father and Mother lived out loud, demonstrating the socialization process of how we should live, and who we should be.

As an adult, I now recognize and believe my parents were very intentional in a natural and unconscious way. Guests in our home were from different countries with different cultures. I recall people coming with different types of food and discussing the ingredients. Whether walking through the neighborhood or during family vacations we learned about respect for others. When I was a child,

Father and Mother would have a map and would have my siblings and me point to a place we wanted to go. We were then instructed to research that selection and give an oral report.

My parents hosted dinner parties or social gatherings, where my siblings and I were expected to hang the guests' coats and even ask if they wanted something to drink. Once the meal was finished my siblings and I would then either sing songs or recite poetry – skills that I have continued as an adult. My worldview as a child was shaped without prejudice, but rather with periodic reminders to "work hard" and remember "whose child you are." My values and beliefs were shaped and demonstrated by the examples of my parents. One vivid memory I have is attending a father-daughter Girl Scout hiking event. While on the trail my sister and I saw a person walking. We began to point and laugh; instantly my father stopped walking and said, "Stop it right now; you don't point and laugh and anybody; you don't ever know what a person has been through." What a sobering, teachable moment. There was silence and then, immediate tears (tears that I messed up and made some-one feel bad). That lesson was a paradigm shift in my life that is the foundation of my empathy toward those who are ostracized and marginalized.

This type of behavior was discouraged and went against our family values and beliefs. What a gift to be given a lesson that affected my primary and secondary socialization. I would soon learn about prejudice from those in the same race when our family moved from Ann Arbor, Michigan, to Muskegon Heights, Michigan. What a culture shock. In an extreme contrast, I was followed home from school, hit with sticks and rocks by classmates who would laugh at the way I spoke. "Why you be talking so proper?" "You must think you a honky." "Y'all Baldwins think you better than us."

Regardless of what my family had, my cultural identity and social-ization would still place me in a category of one who has been marginalized. It has been said that our greatest treasure on earth is our identity in Christ. When we know who we are, we are better able and equipped to function the way God intended. Establishing a strong identity is important. Moreover, much like our identity in Christ, we must know who we are in order to represent the king-dom of God well. Another reason for a strong identity has to do with our personal values. Interestingly, it is necessary to acknowl-edge my personal identity along the way. Thus, I am expected to dig deeper, moving beyond the periphery of distractions, obstacles, self-doubt, and debilitating stress that have surfaced and toward lib-erating freedom from barriers of the past. The process of pushing past the surface has been therapeutic in itself and has further con-firmed not only that I was created in the image of God but that my life has been ordained by God to impact change. "And I am sure of this, that he who began a good work in you will bring it to comple-tion at the day of Jesus Christ." Philippians 1:6, NLT

For generations the question of whether or not leaders are made or born has been debated. However, as I was the firstborn in a family of educators, leadership or being tasked with the responsibilities of a leader was non-negotiable. The development of personal values is the result of an expectation that academic achievement is the key to success. As previously indicated, my mother and father prepared their children through an identity of privilege, with a mantra and instructions that we pay attention to our surroundings and always leave people better than we found them. Mother and Father would further plan family vacations which I now believe doubled as a cultural enrichment experience. Whether at home, work, school, church or in the community we were reminded of who we were, whom we represented, thus shaping and molding our values.

My attitudes, beliefs and values have also been shaped void of prejudice but rather with an awareness that hard work and treating people the way I want to be treated would bring about good things. "So, whatever you wish that others would do to you, do also to them, for this is the Law and the Prophets" Matthew 7:12, NIV. One vivid memory I have is observing my parents prepare meals for families in need and having my siblings and me write note cards to go in the bags before we delivered them. This was a definite act and example of shaping our values through social responsibility. "For I was hungry and you gave me food, I was thirsty and you gave me drink, I was a stranger and you welcomed me, I was naked and you clothed me, I was sick and you visited me, I was in prison and you came to me." Matthew 25:35-36, NIV

Another example was an expectation that my siblings and I read the newspaper as a family, followed by an impromptu oral presentation sharing an overview of the articles we read. I am grateful for the value-shaping formative years, as these values became a lifeline once our family relocated from Ann Arbor, Michigan to Muskegon Heights, Michigan. This move was what I believe to be the beginning of the end of my life of privilege and social harmony. In a new and predominantly African American environment I was bullied, teased, and hit with rocks and sticks for being different, speaking different, acting different—in other words, being raised in a multicultural environment where people carried themselves with dignity and respect regardless of culture, ethnicity or social status. It was also the end of my parents' marriage a few years later. Nonetheless, my personal values were established and just needed to be maintained. The greatest commandment is a reminder of such. "You shall love the Lord your God with all your heart and with all your soul and with all your might. And these words that I command you today shall be on your heart. You shall teach them diligently to your children, and shall talk of them when you sit in your house, and when you walk by the way, and when you lie down, and when you rise" Deuteronomy 6:5-7, ESV. Although I was young, I quickly learned to be careful with the manner in which I spoke and interacted with people. When I was upset, frustrated or felt stressed my tendency was to quiet myself, saying very little if anything.

The rationale behind this behavior is not to speak when in this state of vulnerability. This is where things can be said that will cause harm to the recipient of a quick tongue. Realistically, this is definitely not the norm, as I encountered peers who would lash out with expletives, insults, as well as physical and verbal attacks. During this stage in my traumatic experience, I learned the liberating art of being myself. I learned how to separate the person from their behavior. Mother and Grandmother would often say, "It's just nice to be nice." Even when I didn't want to, their voices still caused me to pause and consider my actions. Likewise, for these reasons I refrain from speaking harshly or using profanity. "Let no corrupting talk come out of your mouths, but only such as is good for building up, as fits the occasion, that it may give grace to those who hear" Ephesians 4:29, NIV. Specifically, I do not believe one should praise God with the same tongue that is used to curse, belittle, demean, or verbally abuse another. Thus, "The good person out of the good treasure of his heart produces good, and the evil person out of his evil treasure produces evil for out of the abundance of the heart his mouth speaks" Luke 6:45, NLT. I learned the importance of conducting myself with the utmost dignity and humility, while avoiding any behaviors and practices that would bring dishonor to God. In addition, I was taught to believe that one person's perception is another person's reality. Furthermore, I believe personal values impact our interaction with others, which is also reflective of our life experiences.

From childhood, whether through hands-on missionary ministry meetings with my grandmother or meal preparation and delivery with my parents, I learned the importance of caring for and nurturing others. "So then, as we have opportunity, let us do good to everyone, and especially to those who are of the household of faith" Galatians 6:10, ESV. Admittedly, my hypocrisy of failing to care adequately for myself is troubling, especially with countless years of adverse situations and circumstances that have often been paralyzing and unbearable. Nonetheless, I ask myself how I can speak to others while still working through my rubble of personal adversity. Each life-transforming experience has a positive effect or challenges us to think, ponder and reconsider our thoughts, actions, influences and effect on our character and well-being. In fact, character is described as what surfaces when no one is looking. This nine-letter word (character) has been etched in my heart and on my mind from childhood to present. Upstanding character therefore means doing the right thing even when I don't want to. God's faithfulness has been my model, especially as it relates to circumstances and situations at each stage of my life. The word of God says, "So let us then approach God's throne of grace with confidence, so that we may receive mercy and find grace to help us in our time of need" Hebrews 4:16, NIV. God's love produces confidence regardless of where we are along life's journey. It is through the power of God that our circumstances, or in many cases our perspective, changes. God's word also says, "Trust in the Lord and do good: dwell in the land and enjoy safe pasture. Take delight in the Lord, and he will give you the desires of your heart. Commit your way to the Lord; trust in him and he will do this; He will make your righteous reward shine like the dawn" Psalm 37:2-6, NIV.

God gives instruction, followed by what he will do upon completion of our obedience. Therefore, regardless of health challenges, struggles, obstacles, setbacks and circumstances far beyond my control, obstacles do not cancel my life assignment. Both personal and professional life experiences have transformed me. Some experiences, although traumatic, have not only been life changing, but also mind-altering encounters that have become a witness to a plethora of priceless moments of God's faithfulness. You too can be a witness. How, you ask? As a believer, you might consider self-assessment by shifting self-talk to hearing from God, especially as the question arises, "Why is this happening to me or why has 'it' not happened for me?"

There has seemingly always been a fire within me, often almost supernaturally fueled in the midst of traumatic life experiences. I attribute this trait to that of my parents, whose compassionate human service-oriented demeanor and commitment as educators would model for my siblings and me to do likewise. I recall hearing comments: "You are wise beyond your years," "You listen and hear everything," "How did you know that?" "You are a different child," Why are you being so nice when 'they' weren't nice to you?" and finally, "I always feel better after talking to you." While the aforementioned comments were ongoing from teachers, family members, adults in general, as well as my peers, I have always felt perplexed, as if I didn't fit in, yet honored that people confide in me. It has always been a privilege to simply listen to those who are challenged and in need of someone to listen and maintain confidentiality.

Sometimes I wonder if my ability to keep quiet would become an accomplice of sorts to the traumatic life experiences that would follow one who has experienced such a vibrant, wholesome foundation, which are revealed now only for the purpose of sharing my motivation and urgency to serve as a clinical mental health counselor. Through life experience and in-depth training to help and heal others through trauma-informed care, others will feel secure in talking things through with me. The revelation of life experiences which have shaped my thinking as well as recollection of times when I needed to talk things through is the primary motivating factor. I needed to talk things through after being inappropriately touched by an elderly family member. I needed to talk things through after being raped by someone who says he (now she) wanted to "teach me a lesson" because I was miss good girl for not following the crowd in school and wanting to save my virginity for marriage. I needed to talk things through after being again inappropriately touched on multiple occasions by a female cousin. I needed to talk things through after being inappropriately touched by a female camp counselor and threatened "not to tell anyone." I needed to talk things through after being expected to care for my siblings since I was the eldest, and expected to discipline my siblings or otherwise be disciplined myself, for not doing so. I needed to talk things through after the divorce of my parents at the formative age of 15, with my father leaving the home, only to return after gaining custody of my twin and two younger brothers. Eventually I would share with my father that I wanted to live with my mother, to which Father responded, "If you go there, I can't trust you." After some time with my mother, I would move back with my father a year later and eventually out on my own at age 17. I needed to talk things through after enduring spousal abuse and abandonment after one year of marriage due to adultery, and persevering through the traumatic experience to raise our son as a single parent. Divorce during the late 1990s was shameful and embarrassing while riddled with ongoing ridicule, rejection and uncertainty. As a result of my own divorce, I needed to talk things through, as I encountered judgment by those in the Christian Reformed Church where I served as minister of music, who would no longer communicate, socialize, or welcome me into their homes after the departure of my former husband.

During these traumatic times, God's hand would continue to guide me, counsel me, insulate me and prepare me for a triumphant entry of sorts into the realm of a higher plateau. In this regard, and for as long as I can coherently remember, I have been an advocate for those who are different. Whether seeing them through the lens of their appearance, personality, perspectives, or idiosyncrasies, I have been endowed with a gift of looking past, around and beyond the challenges and obstacles of others and simply seeing their need. This awareness has developed throughout my formative years, and continues to do so today. By God's unfailing grace and mercy, my life purpose of empowering, encouraging and equipping others to live a life of excellence is the result of being transformed by God's faithfulness. Just as the Israelites were set apart and regarded as a peculiar people, I have been set aside to serve as God's hand extended in the world and as an agent of his love to the nations. "Before I formed you in the womb I knew you, and before you were born I consecrated you: I appointed you a prophet to the nations" Jeremiah 1:5, ESV. The choices we make today affect our tomorrow. Therefore, our today is a result of our decisions made yesterday. The book of Joshua is a reminder that God is a God of second chances. The Israelites wasted 40 years because of their lack of faith. In like manner, I have been given an opportunity to complete that which has been on and in my mind, body, and spirit for 40 years. "Now therefore fear the Lord and serve him in sincerity and in faithfulness, and choose this day whom you will serve" Joshua 24: 14-15, ESV. I am compelled to "press on toward the goal for the prize of the upward call of God in Christ Jesus" Philippians 3:14, ESV.

Regardless of challenges situations, or obstacles, attaining an education is a priceless achievement that can never be taken, erased, or dissolved. Unfortunately, I have faced professional trauma from relocating to a place where my education has been ignored, overlooked, disregarded and looked down upon. The result has been workplace bullying, through which I have once again persevered, regardless of countless attempts to discourage and dissuade me considering advancement. This is evident by the plethora of employment opportunities for which I have been intentionally overlooked.

Because of my refusal to compromise my integrity through unethical practices, I have experienced being either blacklisted or patronizingly assured that I am overqualified. This is both significant and perplexing, because I come from a family of educators who have been incessant about the benefit of a "good education." My experience, however, is quite the opposite and has set the foundation for extreme financial debt for higher education through postgraduate studies. Yet, my work is far from what I ever considered. It can be and has been disheartening to watch helplessly, while others are selected and recommended for job opportunities that either have the exact experience and credentials or neither. This lens of carnal immaturity briefly caused self-doubt, which sought to taint all that I have sacrificed. As I become more seasoned, I am learning the importance of acceptance, forgiveness, and grace, personally and professionally. What I have experienced and perceived as trauma has prepared and is preparing me for my time, my chance, my opportunity. Nonetheless, I have come to realize that I have been waiting for that which I already possess. God's faithfulness in my life has transformed me from the empty and hollow abyss of trying to prove myself as the eldest child of my parents, as a believer in Christ Jesus, as student, as a sibling, as a wife, as a mother and as myself. Often, I ask myself why I think it is necessary to always make sure everyone is taken care of, feels accepted, included, forgiven and as if they matter, are significant and valuable. In this regard, there have been traumatic life experiences that God continues to transform into a triumphant journey. What an honor to be used as God's instrument of praise.

Early in my life as a new Christian I recall naively praying a heartfelt plea: "Lord, use me for your service, and I will be careful to give you the glory and honor you deserve; in the name of Jesus I pray. Amen." **As a child**, we learn to please and appease our parents so as not to disappoint our parents, guardians, adult figures, and life influences. **As a sibling**, we learn to share and be fair in order to keep peace. As an only child we are the only one there, with no other to compare. **As a student**, I vividly recall the expectation of my parents that homework was a priority as my only job was that of a student. Interestingly, this was a priceless moment as it shaped my work ethic and sparked a desire to teach, inform and thrive as a lifelong learner. One of my fondest memories is attending a Catholic high school. Because of the costly tuition my mother, a professional musician, teacher, preacher and education advocate for her children arranged to pay for tuition through a system of bartering.

I would be dropped off at the convent where the sister (nun) would greet me with a list of tasks to be completed that particular Saturday morning. Once cleaning was complete, we would share a meal together. Finally, we would make our way to an acoustic sound and picturesque studio, where I would receive piano lessons. This special time would last for several years and is etched on my heart as a priceless moment of God's faithfulness. The peace, quiet tranquility, reverence and awareness of God's presence appealed to me and by no prompting other than the Holy

Spirit I was drawn to thoughts of dedication to religious service as a nun. These thoughts would be stored away, as I would eventually marry, and eventually divorce.

As a friend, we learn how to be there or beware. **As the romantic interest of another,** we learn that we must love ourselves and be open and accepting of ourselves in order to do the same for another. We must ensure that our needs are met while striving to do for another. Unfortunately, more often than not we might admit our effort is nonreciprocal. Oh, how God must feel when we seek him for what he can do for us rather than who he is. Oh, it must break God's heart that we lament after individuals who are not worth our time, effort and salvation. Yet we continue to create a pseudo-something, that is anything but what and who God has individually designed, specifically, intricately and individually designated. And once again we cry out to God, creator of the universe and ultimate lover of our soul. Oh, how God must grieve as we take him for granted in the same manner as those to whom we give all that belongs to and should be given back to God. Lord, help us to become who you have created us to be. "For we are His workmanship, created in Christ Jesus for good works, which God prepared beforehand so that we would walk in them." We belong to God.

Finally, as a wife I vividly recall my perception that marriage was a team effort whereby couples worked to ensure the best interest of their spouse. I so admired my parents and grandparents. Marriage in my mind was something to aspire to, whether cooking, cleaning, washing, sewing, or nurturing children. As an example, the character of a Proverbs 31 woman was to be emulated, along with the older women of the church, many times to include the pastor's wife. Marriage was an institution, a privilege and an honor. Little girls are programmed to believe if they follow the proper steps with poise and posture while saving virginity for marriage, they will hit the jackpot, metaphorically speaking. Being a wife was mentioned and alluded to more and more as I advanced through my high school years. Yet I was content working in the school library and completing my course curriculum to graduate in the spring, as did all high school seniors. While minding my own business, as I always have, I began to notice a young man who would study in the library, checking out books and often asking questions about the genres of literature. The questions and need for assistance became more and more frequent. Eventually we would become attached and marry.

Without warning I was thrust into the realm of being a single parent due to spousal abandonment just under one year into the marriage. This traumatic experience was the catalyst for where the Lord is using me. My purpose is clear and there is no doubt that a mighty purpose has been entrusted to me to fulfill. Not surprisingly, I have questioned whether or not God is pleased. Although I possess the passion, I wonder if I have mastered the assignment, as obstacles do not cancel our assignments. Living a sacrificial life before the Lord is evident by the scriptures that I apply, to ensure that at the appointed time I will prayerfully hear the Lord say, "Well done, thy good and faithful servant."

Prayerfully the following scriptures will encourage you as you recognize how God's individualized grace and mercy will transform your trials into a testimony of priceless moments through his faithfulness:

"His divine power has granted to us all things that
pertain to life and godliness, through the knowledge
of him who called us to his own glory and excellence
given us everything required for life and godliness

through the knowledge of Him who called us
by His own glory and godliness"
2 Peter 1:3, ESV

"Commit to the Lord whatever you do, and He will
establish your plans."
Proverbs 16:3, ESV

"What one person does affects another, Hence:
God's word, how can two walk together unless
they are agreed?"
Amos 3:3, NIV

"If the two of you shall agree on earth as touching anything they shall ask, it shall be done for them."
Matthew 18:19, NLT

"So let us then approach God's throne of grace with
confidence, so that we may receive mercy and find
grace to help us in our time of need."
Hebrews 4:16, NIV

God's love produces confidence regardless of where we are along
life's journey. It is through the power of God that our circumstances, or in many cases our perspective, change.

"Trust in the Lord and do well, dwell in the land and
enjoy safe pasture. Take delight in the Lord, and he will
give you the desires of your heart. Commit your way to
the Lord; trust in him and he will do this; He will make
your righteous reward shine like the dawn."
Psalm 37:2-6, NIV

God's faithfulness has been and is a balm of healing. I am filled with gratitude for the privilege to serve God with my life, by serving his people. Let us be mindful that everyone has a story; let us refrain from belittling, slandering and assuming what we think we know about another person. Let us refrain from referring to town gossips and entertaining ongoing conversations with those who hold malicious and ill intent against people they know nothing about, other than skewed perceptions, which are viewed through a cracked lens. Be encouraged and mindful that God gives instruction, followed by what he will do upon completion of our obedience. It is through quiet introspection that I am healed, healing, and recognizing daily a gift given to me, which is a lifetime of priceless moments through God's faithfulness.

Pamela Nance Johnson, born in Okinawa, Japan; now resides in Fredericksburg, Virginia. Pamela spent most of her career in service to others. Her positions at the local Head Start program and Rappahannock Area Community Services Board allowed her to advocate for area children and families. She also served as an AmeriCorps VISTA (Volunteers in Service to America) through the Corporation for National and Community Service and a Court Appointed Special Advocate for children. Since 2012, she been employed by the federal government, her current position is Legal Administrative Specialist.

Pamela serves in ministry as a member of Kingdom Family Worship Center where she was ordained as Minister in 2015. She serves in music ministry, Sunday school and the church administration team. She has been frequently featured as a guest blogger for Hope-in-Christ Ministries. Pamela Nance Johnson seeks to use her testimony to encourage others in their faith journey.

Pamela Nance Johnson

Free Indeed

Pamela Nance Johnson

Jesus replied, "Very truly I tell you, everyone who sins is a slave to sin. 35 Now a slave has no permanent place in the family, but a son belongs to it forever. 36 So if the Son sets you free, you will be free indeed." John 8:34, NIV

Certainly, I'd read that scripture passage and heard sermons based on the text many times in my life. The emphasis was mostly on verse 36 and that's what I longed for, freedom—the kind of freedom that is "indeed" true and absolute.

It would take almost twenty years and a heart-wrenching experience for me to put my life's journey on paper and let others into my world. I knew that sharing my testimony would bring up old feelings of hurt but give me strength to let them go. I wanted to encourage others who may be in a similar situation. Why now? I had dreamed of becoming a published author since childhood. I loved to read and wanted to one day have my name listed on the pages of a book. It's truly amazing how God worked it out. I was searching the Internet for a writing conference that would focus on Christian books. I came upon the Christian Book Lover's Retreat in Charlotte, North Carolina. I attended for the first time in October 2017, and I knew right away that God had surely ordered my steps.

I was challenged for the next two years to start writing. As I read the guidelines for the 2019 *Back in the Day* anthology, I thought this would be my literary gateway. The theme was for writers to share encouraging stories of deliverance. Since I didn't consider myself a storyteller, I wouldn't be able to use fictional characters. I'd have to stand in my truth and reveal it, just as it had happened. I was ready to write, but I was afraid of what my family would say or feel toward me. I didn't know how my ex would react if he ever read or heard about it. My first few pages began to flow rather well until something happened that caused me to almost give up completely.

On Palm Sunday, March 25, 2018 my three sons, ages 32, 30 and 17, were returning home to Virginia from a weekend visit with their father and siblings in North Carolina. They had gone to celebrate their father's birthday. My mother's intuition told me that something was not quite right, but I had no idea what it was. I had attended worship service at my church earlier that morning. I was ready to return for the evening service of The Seven Last Sayings of Christ, where I was to serve as an Expeditor. I expected their return in the afternoon, when my oldest son Brian drove down and would drop his brothers off before he went home. When he entered, he hesitated, then my youngest son, Aaron, came in and the expression on his face spoke volumes. Where was my middle child, Antonio? He came into the house and I saw his face red and swollen. I could hardly speak—what in the world happened and why didn't anyone call me? My oldest son began to explain that the night before, they had all gone to what I call a juke joint or hole in the wall club. At some point a scuffle or fight was about to break out and they were trying to get away from the chaos. In those types of places, there is usually one way in and one way out. My sons were supposedly with family, but they were very much outsiders in that environment. Apparently, the family got separated but Aaron had made it to the car. Antonio was on his way to the car when he was confronted by a dude with a gun. He stood between the car, while his younger brother was crouched down in the seat, and the gunman attacked him. Antonio was hit in the face with the gun. I asked if he'd gone to the hospital. Not initially—they went to their sister's house, then later to the local hospital in NC for some triage and basic assessment. The fact that not one of the siblings or their father bothered to pick up a cell phone and call or text me to say anything at all about this made me angry and my heart ached for my son. I told Brian to take Antonio to our local hospital. I think I was in a state of shock because I couldn't cry but I felt the tears and then rage welling up inside of me. It's like when you want to cry out but there's no sound.

I had given my usual safety talk before they left. I had prayed and since I hadn't heard anything, I hoped all was well. I knew that they would gather for a family dinner or something then go out somewhere. I had asked where Aaron would stay. They said he was staying with the younger children and I had insisted, so I thought that would be the plan. However, I was told that since a teenage niece came along, everyone basically said Aaron should also. As a safeguard, Aaron was given the keys so he could go directly to the car if anything went wrong. Well, it was wrong for him to even be there at all. I wondered how the turn of events had affected him as he sat crouched down in the car and could hear his brother being attacked right outside. Naturally, Aaron was afraid but instead of calling me, he called a friend. I was glad he had someone to reach out to, even if it wasn't me. The more I heard, the sadder and then the more filled with anger and rage I became. I was angry that despite their intentions to celebrate, no one was the voice of reason. Not even their father had considered the consequences or accepted any responsibility for this disaster. My ex didn't even reach out to tell me that our sons were on their way home, but something had gone terribly wrong, that Antonio was injured. It was then that I felt like I didn't want to continue writing. I felt powerless. How could I encourage anyone else to overcome their circumstances in my condition?

Well, I did go on to church on Palm Sunday evening, but I didn't speak a word of what had just taken place in my home. I was there physically and I even enjoyed portions of the service. However, my mind was across town. When I got home, I was told that Antonio's jaw was in fact broken and he'd need surgery. He was able to get the treatment done at a teaching hospital an hour away from our home. Antonio had to have his jaw wired and was only able to have liquids for several weeks. He lost a lot of weight and I know he tried to keep his spirits up, but it was a difficult time for us. Aaron didn't talk much about it but said he would be okay. Brian wanted to pursue a formal complaint with law enforcement in NC. All the while, I still heard nothing from my ex. It wasn't until Aaron was on a college visit in Raleigh, NC that my ex reached out and asked why we hadn't told him about the tour. Aaron was participating in a Junior Day football event. The last thing we needed was a distraction. I didn't want the past to affect our future. I knew Antonio had been healed when he gave me permission to share his story as part of my testimony for this project. I thank God for that act of deliverance. God has been better than good to us.

I'd left my ex before Aaron was born. I thought that when I left, I was free, but children kept us connected. I shared in the *Back in the Day* anthology how I would make my exit while the world was in frenzy at the notion of Y2K. A few people even predicted the world would end. While their focus was on that milestone, I wondered a couple of things, one being what part of "no one knows" did they not understand (Matthew 24:36, NIV)? Second, how could I make my departure from this marriage at this pivotal time in history? I was praying for a new beginning. The possibility of a Y2K computer glitch was the furthest thing from my mind.

It felt like I couldn't even breathe. I was walking on eggshells, just waiting to hear them crack and all hell break loose. This was not the life I or my children deserved. My prayer was "God, change the situation or give me a way of escape." I watched and waited for things to get better, but nothing changed. In fact, a few things got worse. I was desperate and when I began to listen to His voice, I saw God working in my life like never before.

So many times I grew up hearing how a woman could do bad by herself. I know that the people who used that phrase meant that you don't need help from another person to do badly or fail miserably in life; you can do that alone. Yes, that is very true in and of itself. But I was raised to be a "good" girl.

I met my ex soon after Brian was born. I was working at a local McDonald's. At first, I didn't pay much attention to his flirting. I wasn't going to get caught up with this man who was nearly ten years older than me. But he was smooth and persistent; I started to develop an interest.

He was a truck driver and of course I'd heard things like they have women in every city they visit. I had a few reservations in the beginning, but I chose to ignore them. I saw what appeared to be a handsome, hard-working, kind man who grew on my family and embraced my son. The woman's intuition and the red flags just faded. At first, I thought there was no way I was going out with this country boy. I was a city girl. When he told me he had four children by four different women, I should have run the other way. I should have heard The Temptations song "Papa Was A Rolling Stone" playing in my head. The first line of that song would become quite familiar. Why did I think it would be any different for me? Why would I want to be number five? Maybe I thought I could help him to change—big mistake. We were on totally different courses in life.

Before I knew it, seven years had gone by and we had a son together. I had even left once and moved in with another family member. I was either longsuffering or a glutton for punishment because I went back. I knew he was seeing other women. It was clear that I wasn't the only one. I still wanted things to work out, though. I know we both liked the idea of marriage but there was really no foundation there. After seven years of living together, we got married. Why did we get married? I can definitely relate to the Tyler Perry movie titles. I suppose I just wanted to have a real family and I believed my ex-husband did too. He would brag about his children. He loved them but it just didn't seem as though he wanted to raise them. Driving a truck was his escape from the responsibilities of parenthood. He wasn't taking care of his children and I knew at least one of the children's mothers had filed for child support in another state. Once, I answered the door and a female sheriff served child support papers. I thought she was out of line when she asked if my sons were his children. She said, "He's not taking care of his other kids and probably won't take care of yours, either." I was angry then a bit sad. She was right. I never told anyone about that short exchange, but I never forgot it, either.

By this time, it was maybe 1993 and one of my stepdaughters, age 14, had come to live with us. We had truly become a blended family. I didn't know that it wouldn't be long before I was not only a stepmother but a grandmother as well. I decided that I would be the best role model and support I could. I knew what she was going through because I had gone through a pregnancy alone. We had a family meeting where I told my husband's sisters I didn't need them to come to the rescue. I wouldn't be sending my step-daughter to live with them; we'd get through it together, and we did. Our new addition was a healthy, beautiful baby girl. I have no regrets and am glad I was able to be there.

During the summer that my stepdaughter came to live with us, I found my way back to church. In the strip mall near our apartment complex was a store-front church. I had seen the pastor, his wife and his family a few times from a distance. One day I asked if they had Vacation Bible School. I don't remember if they did but I started by sending the children to Sunday School. Soon I started going to a few services myself. At first, I felt bad because I didn't have nice dresses to wear. In the days of layaway, I'd use what money I had for school clothes or Christmas gifts. Money was tight and I had to make do.

Dress clothes or not, I attended that church, and I developed a relationship with one of the Church Mothers. She gave me a few dresses. This Prayer Warrior encouraged me and offered wisdom at a time when I was trying to find my way back to God. I would later find out that we had more in common than I knew. I began to go to church more, and I rededicated my life to God. I had accepted Jesus Christ as my Savior years ago but had strayed so far away from what I knew. One of the Sisters would pick me up and we'd go to other services. On one occasion, a young preacher reminded me that God is married to the Backslider. I was in tears and knew then that I could get back to the place where I first believed.

I started to volunteer at my sons' school and served on the Parent Council. I found that if I occupied my time with church and community activities I could cope with the situation. When a position for a Teacher's Assistant became available, one of my son's teachers suggested I apply for the position. She is a Prayer Warrior and Songbird too. God was ordering my steps, whether I recognized it or not. I applied for the position, had an interview with a city school official and got the job. It changed my life. I could hardly believe it. I didn't have an Early Childhood degree. I was just a volunteer mother. I didn't accept that others would see potential in me. I started a career at the local Head Start as a Teacher's Assistant and Bus Monitor. Although I didn't have a driver's license or a car, God had already worked it out. As a Bus Monitor I could go the elementary school with my son and transfer to my Head Start route. I gained a greater appreciation for teachers and support staff. While I had volunteered at the school sometimes, it was very different from managing a classroom full of three-year-old children. I loved the Head Start program, but honestly, I wasn't a teacher. Again, God stepped in. The following year, our program was awarded funding for two Family Service Worker positions. The FSW would assist with recruitment, eligibility, and enrollment. In addition, they would develop family partnerships and identify local community resources. Yes, I applied for one of the positions and became one of the first FSW in our program. Once again, God showed favor. I didn't have a degree in social work, only my limited classroom experience and resourceful instincts. This position would give me a chance to share with others the knowledge and tools to reach goals beyond their child's preschool education.

At Head Start we were to make home visits as a component of the family partnership. I needed to be mobile. A family friend gave me driving lessons after I got my learner's permit. Meanwhile, my church changed locations and was no longer in walking distance. I remember being so proud of myself when I got the driver's license. I could drive myself to work and church. I could drive myself to the grocery store or wherever else we needed to go. I gained a new sense of independence.

While I was taking advantage of training and professional development at Head Start, I began to build my resume and seek more responsibility. Our family settled into a single-family house in an established community. My ex was working off and on. It seemed that there was always an issue that caused him to leave a job. While I really liked my job, it certainly wasn't enough money to support the household. He had bought a second car for me at some point. It was a cute, red Hyundai. When we couldn't make the payments, it was repossessed. I remember getting ready for work one morning. I looked out in the driveway where I had parked the night before and the car was not there. I wanted to cry; I probably did cry. I had to call someone from work to pick me up. Thank God we lived close to the school. I had to explain the situation to my supervisor. It was so embarrassing. I thought if the car payments weren't made then the mortgage wasn't either. It was only a matter of time before we'd be in foreclosure or worse. How could I let that happen? I was dealing with the infidelity in my marriage but that wasn't what caused me to act. It was the possibility of being homeless. After the car was repossessed, I got a part time job at a local grocery store to earn extra money. In a few months I paid cash for a little used car. It wasn't much but I had earned the money and it was mine. I drove that little Pontiac Sunbird until I could do better.

It was at this point that I started to think about separation. I wanted out of this situation. If things were not going to get better, I had to make a decision. I had endured 14 years; however, I was not going to live 14 more years the same way. After all, my job was to locate resources for others. God always has a plan and gave me guidance once again. The saying "charity begins at home" began to mean more to me. How could I help others and not myself and my children? As I was working with families living in a certain housing complex, I was told that there was a management change in process and several families were moving. I set up a meeting with the management staff and applied for housing there. I asked the staff not to contact me at home, only at work.

Once I was approved for an apartment, I told my ex. He was in denial, but I wasn't. He had no idea what I'd been working on. I moved in silence. I realize most women stay in situations for the children. However, that wasn't me. I wanted a better life for us. If that meant leaving, then that's what I'd do. I decided that it didn't matter if I ever got an apology, I'd move on. I was standing on the promise that my latter would be greater, as in Job 8:7. I told my pastor that I wouldn't be the church wife who stayed until death, not in this case. I appreciate their struggle, but I was tired of enduring that lifestyle. I didn't think God wanted me to stay in an unhealthy marriage. God didn't look too kindly on adultery or infidelity.

I told my sons that this housing situation was only temporary. Ironically, this was the same low-income housing that I had considered so many years ago. That first night in the small two-bedroom apartment, I took a look around and felt more peace than I had in a long time. I had two teenage sons and a recently confirmed pregnancy with my third child, but I was determined that I would not go back. It was still a struggle at times, but God showed Himself strong in my life every step of the way. I learned to work while I waited for guidance and direction. I kept the faith and drew closer to God. I was becoming a Prayer Warrior myself. I had started working with the youth in church and joined the choir. It was a joy to work with the teen Sunday School class. After nearly two years, I applied for a house through our local Habitat for Humanity program and was approved. It would take prayer, hours of sweat equity and volunteer service before we moved into our three-bedroom house. It was a blessing that only God could provide: I was a homeowner. Imagine that—look at God! A couple years later I filed for a divorce and gained a new sense of direction, willing to follow God's lead.

In 2019, I would come full circle on my quest toward freedom. I hadn't spoken to my ex in over a year. However, the connection of our children would be the catalyst for me to finally give voice to the sound that had been silent within me. As Aaron's high school graduation approached one weekend, Brian's wedding would be the following weekend. My ex called me, and I decided to answer. He got straight to the point, asking if I had a problem with him. I decided then, yes, I'd take back my power. I would no longer be a victim, afraid to speak my truth. I told my ex, yes, I indeed had a problem and for once he would listen and not talk over me. I let him know that after what happened on his birthday weekend in 2018, I had lost any respect for him as a father. How could he put my children (no matter their ages) in harm's way and say nothing or accept no responsibility at all? How dare he? I was no longer afraid and let him know it. I just wanted him to leave me alone. I just didn't want to be bothered. At the graduation, we sat with other family in between us. At the wedding, we were escorted separately. I made it clear that I didn't want fake pictures or small talk. I was done but certainly didn't want to ruin either event for my children. God kept me through it all.

I am in no way advocating divorce or offering marital counseling. My intent was not to blame the whole situation on my ex-husband either. I made mistakes, too, and accept my responsibility and the part I played in the marriage that failed. If I had not gone through these trials or tests, I would not have a testimony to share. I wouldn't be able to encourage other women in similar situations. A young girl who has lost her mother can see that God will send Mothers and Sister-friends to give wise counsel, practical tips, and prayer. A single mother can realize that with God she is not raising her children alone. A woman who needs to leave a relationship can know that there is life after divorce.

My purpose is to share that even in a dark situation, if you put your trust in God, He will deliver you and work on your behalf. I learned to pray for myself and listen as God spoke through people. When He opened doors, I had to move not in fear but in faith. I learned that God still works miracles. These days I use scripture, songs, and prayer to encourage myself and others. I choose to be victorious, no longer a victim. Here I am in 2021, stepping into new areas as an author and blogger. I've decided to take full advantage of every opportunity when God opens doors. I know that as Proverbs 18:16, NKJV says, "A man's gift makes room for him and brings him before great men" .

I know that I am more than a conqueror through Him who loved me (Romans 8:27). With God, I can make it through anything. I know that my life is so much better with God on my side and nearly twenty years later, I am free indeed.

Mona Lisa Griffin is the founder and CEO of H.O.P.E (Healing Over Paralyzed Emotions) They help pre-teens and women overcome feelings of hopelessness, neglect, and abandonment issues that were brought on by being raised by a toxic parent.

They also help their clients to uncover the feelings and emotions that have kept them paralyzed. Equipping them to be Anchored and to stand in Hope, that joy will come in the morning.

Mona is also a Certified Transformational Life Coach, Author and Motivational Speaker. She is a Native of Grand Rapid, MI, born and raised. She has one daughter Ja'Mya who is her pride and joy.

From Broken Pieces to Peace

Mona Griffin

"Why Lord? What do you want from me?" is what I screamed at the top of my lungs on a winter day in December 2019, at the top of Lookout Mountain in my hometown of Grand Rapids, MI. On that particular day it was not in my plans to be up there, I was to be by a body of water where I would commit suicide. Two hours earlier I had walked into my daughter's room and looked around. She was at work. With tears in my eyes, I told her that I loved her and not to let anyone tell her any different. Why did I get to that point in my life? Allow me to take you back.

As far back as I can remember, I recall my life being wonderful, up until the tender age of six. You see, I was a momma's girl, all the way from head to toe. My mother was my idol and I was her little girl. My mother was a single parent and at that time, I was the youngest, with an older brother. My brother was my best friend, and I followed him a lot because we were close in age. I am talking from jumping off roofs to jumping trains and all of that. We had a lot of fun back then, even with the kids in our neighborhood. Well, my happiness and the atmosphere all changed when my little sister was born and I instantly became the middle child.

In addition, of course, like any other child, you are mad that all the attention is on the baby and not you, so I felt some type of way. However, I was not just feeling it but also showing it. This is when the separation began, because I felt I was in competition for my mother's attention and love. I really felt the separation when we would all be sitting at the table to eat. I was a really picky eater. I just didn't like a lot of the food that my mother prepared, but we would be at the table laughing and just conversing and me playing in my food, as the grown folks would say, not knowing that I would have to finish all my food before I got up from the table. Dad would take my sister out of her chair; of course, my brother would finish because he wanted to get back to his Atari game. My mom would get up and tell me, "You're not leaving this table until you've finished your food." The first time that happened, I was so sad because I was alone in the kitchen and I just stuffed the food down. It made me so sick that I would go to the bathroom and throw up—yes, at six years old. It got to the point where I wasn't going to keep making those trips to the bathroom, so what did I do? I found an empty cabinet in the kitchen that my mother never used and when they would get up from the table, I would scrape my food in that cabinet and wait like 15 minutes, then run in the living room saying, "I finished my plate, Mom." Well, of course, it had to be confirmed so my dad would come check it out. The first place he looked was the garbage and, in the sink, and of course, he found nothing. I dodged an ass-whooping that night. Well, let's just say I tried my luck again and it worked; they found nothing. Hell, this became a game to me at this point up until we started to get roaches and mice. My mother is a very neat and clean woman, so this was out for her. She searched high and low then BAM! She came across that drawer. I had to have been dumping for a least two months. The first person's name she yelled was mine, and I had to clean that mildew-infested cabinet out and got my ass tore up. After that, I really had to eat my food but I just resorted back to throwing up, and I did all that because I didn't want to be left by myself at the kitchen table; I wanted to be a part of them, never knowing that years later that would become an underlying trauma that I would have to heal from: separation anxiety.

During this age I was in kindergarten, and I loved school. Ms. Vandyke was my teacher. I loved her. She was really nice and sweet to all the students in her class. The end of the year came and I was told that I would not be going to the next grade—that I had to repeat kindergarten because my mother said that I was slow and that I needed to do another year. I didn't understand at that time because I didn't feel slow. Hell, I colored well in the lines and tied my shoes right, and knew all my ABCs, but at that time I was just happy that I got another year with my favorite teacher.

Each year after that my mother kept saying to me, "You're slow; you can't do this or that"—yeah, granted, I had trouble spelling and reading like all the other kids but with support and encouragement, I know I could have gotten past that point, but with my mother telling me all the time that I couldn't and me believing every word that came out of her mouth—because let's face it, as a little girl that idolized my mother, there was nothing that she could say or do that I wouldn't believe. She was my god before I even knew who God was, like most kids. So, after so many "you can't do this" and "you can't do that", "you're not smart like the other kids" or "you can't catch on like them," I stopped trying because I just knew my mother was right. This is where my depression came in.

I remember sitting in class, and back then we had split classes where we would have to read in front of the class. The purple book was for the advanced readers, the red book was the average readers and the green was for the slower readers. I remember watching the advanced readers, just wishing that I could read like that, but my momma said I couldn't so I was so sad and embarrassed, I felt like a nobody. My mother never encouraged me to do better; all I ever did was take more tests and fail and prove to everybody and my mother that they were right, but in actuality, I had given up on myself. I didn't even try anymore. I was so depressed that I would hide in the bathrooms at school and when I got home, I would dig the scabs off the sores on my legs. My legs were ugly; Mom told me that all the time. I would get an ass whooping because of the blood that was on my sheets from when I woke up. I did not know what depression was; all I knew was I was sad a lot, especially in school. My outlet was running track. I loved Track and Field. That was life to me. I ran all the time, every chance I got, up and down the street, racing my friends all the time. I know they got tired of my ass wanting to race but whatever, because they did not know the life I was living behind closed doors and running was my escape and my freedom. I had won many ribbons on Track and Field days at school. This was the only day I anticipated for the whole school year, and even throughout the school years, hearing my mother say that I couldn't do this or that, I knew for a fact this was something that I could do, and do well. Every year I won first or second place, nothing under. I was so proud of myself. But, looking back, my mother was never at any of my races to see me run and when I got home to tell her, it was like she didn't give a damn at all. All I got was a dry-ass "that's good" but hey, I took it.

One summer I got the surprise of my life. We had those summer programs for the kids in the neighborhood, where we got those free lunches—they were the bomb, too—but we had a track and field day and I ran off course and one of the counselors—we'll call him Mr. Mike—came to me and asked, "Do you know how fast you ran?" I knew I was fast, but the way he was making it seem was like I was Florence Griffith (Flo Jo), the best female track star of all times...to me, anyway. I wanted to be just like her, and he made it seem like I was her. He said they were having a meet down at the college and I should run. I never ran on a real track, only grass and in the streets, so I begged him to go ask my mom. He did and with a lot of begging from me, she said yes. That day came and I walked on that real track field, and I knew that was where I belonged.

Mr. Mike had signed me up for the running long jump and the 50-yard dash; I did not place in the running jump, which was cool because that was not my thing. However, baby, when it was time to line up for the 50-yard dash, when they popped that gun, I was out and all I kept thinking was I had to get to that line first. I took a quick peek over my shoulder to see if anybody was on me. I saw this other black girl on my heels, and baby, when I turned back to look straight, I left her in my dust. I had won and heard my name on those loud speakers: "MONA GRIFFIN takes first." I couldn't believe it. I knew this was what I wanted to do for the rest of my life, but for sure in college. They came to give me my first-place ribbon and told me I qualified to run in the Hershey meet in Pennsylvania. I couldn't believe it; so many people were coming up to me telling me how fast I ran and congratulating me, except the one person that I cared the world for, my mom. She was home so I was so happy when I got there. I jumped out of the car before it stopped completely. I ran in the house where my mom was washing dishes. I was jumping all around and Mr. Mike came in behind me to tell my mom what an amazing job I did and that he would accompany me to Pennsylvania for the Hershey meet. My mom seemed like she was interested and told Mr. Mike she would let him know. As soon as Mr. Mike left, she looked at me—I'll never forget—and said, "You ain't going and don't ask me again." My heart dropped to floor and I started crying because this was my dream, it was a flat-out stern NO... my own mother broke my heart and shattered my dreams and that just took me back into the mindset of "I can't do anything," like she said. I wasn't even smart enough to run track.

At the age of 12, I got my period in school. I remember like it was yesterday. My friend told me that I had something red on the back of my pants. The class was in the middle of quiet time—you know, when we had to put our heads down on the desk when the class was acting up. I raised my hand to go to the bathroom and ran out of the class, went to the bathroom and saw what my friend was talking about, and I was instantly scared because I had no clue what was going on with my body. Good thing we lived right across the street from the school. I ran out of the building and straight home. My mother was there because she worked second shift at that time. I was banging on the door for her to let me in. "Momma," I was screaming. She came to the door. "I'm bleeding down there. Something's wrong. I need to go to the hospital." She looked at me and said, "Girl, go on upstairs, wash up and put this on." She threw me a big-ass mattress pad and told me to go lie down. My mother never told me about my body and what to expect when my body started to change. I did not know anything about my body until Sex Education in sixth grade.

I didn't know about deodorant until like 12. I would walk past my mother; she would grab me and smell me, then smack me or push me and tell me I stank and to go wash up, never once sitting me down to explain to me about my body and the changes my body would be going through. She punished me for something that I did not know about. Then the name calling started. The first time she called me a bitch I was 12. I can't remember what I had done to make her use those words toward me, but I can tell you exactly how it made me feel. I felt so low, as if she spat in my face—hell, she might as well have because that was the worst internal pain I had ever felt, but I did not stop. I was called bitch so often I thought that was my middle name. Whenever she got mad or felt like I wasn't doing something right it just rolled off her tongue, so smooth and without a care in the world, never thinking about how that affected me.

After so long it became normal and I became a bully. I wanted to cuss her out or hit her like she would do me but I couldn't so I picked my target, the weakest kids at school, and bullied them. It made me feel good that I could boss somebody around and cuss them out like my mother did me. It was not right but it was my release. I just sensed that for whatever reason my mother didn't like me and that bothered me, I did everything exactly how she wanted when she wanted, but it was never good enough, and I would sink deeper in depression but I wouldn't tell her because anytime I went to her about anything it would get turned around and I would end up getting my ass beat, cussed or judged, so I just kept everything to myself.

My high school years were not any better. I had a 3.5 GPA in the first half of the ninth grade. I worked hard for this GPA because I wanted to prove to my mom that I could do it even though all those years she said I couldn't, and I had another chance at my dream to run track again too. But that fantasy of mine didn't last long; she made it clear that she didn't have extra and not to ask. So when Ms. Carter, the track coach, told me she wanted me for her team because she heard about me running, I didn't even bother to ask because I already knew what the answer would be.

That's when I started smoking weed and skipping school and just becoming bitter and angry. Why couldn't she just let me be great? What was it about me that she didn't like? I just didn't get it. I hated going home after school because first, I was so angry with her but more so because I never knew what mood she would be in. When I did finally make it home after school, I would do my chores and go straight to sleep because I just did not want to deal with her moods. At night I would be up. That was my peaceful time, without all the yelling and cussing, and I tried to stay out of her way so she wouldn't get mad about something and beat my ass for whatever reason, so I tried my best to avoid her as much as I could.

I was the middle child, so I felt invisible most of the time because she catered more to my younger sibling. Like the saying goes, the youngest gets away with murder and you're left to take the charge. So at 16 I was tired of feeling like I wasn't shit to my mother and my sibling did nothing wrong. It was like she would always put us in competition with one another, so I ran away because I wanted my mother to look for me. That was the worst mistake I could have made. During those two days of me being gone I was raped. It was brutal. I was raped by three men and when they were done with me, they threw me in the alley like I was garbage. I ended up at the hospital and I begged the doctors not to call my mother because this wasn't the way I wanted her to find me. I was strapped down to the bed. It took four nurses to hold me down because my body went into shock. When my mother walked in that room, I felt like I died. I did die; my spirit was gone, but it wasn't what happened to me that night—it was what she said. She walked in and leaned over the bed—I can still smell her breath to this day—and said, "That's what the fuck you get." I felt my spirit leave my body and enter a black hole in my heart. That was the worst day of my life.

When we got home, I cried all night long. My thighs were swollen from the rape. My back was so sore because they raped me on the basement floor. The next day we went to my cousin's house, the one that was with me, so my mother could find out what happened. The lies she told were crazy. I stopped talking to my cousins for years after that, but the crazy part is that to this day my mother has never asked me what happened. She always went off what she heard. Two days later I was back in school, swollen thighs and all. I had to act like none of that had ever taken place, and on top of that my mother told me that if I didn't graduate, the day I was supposed to walk the stage I would be getting the fuck out of her house. Can you imagine being raped and having to put that in the back of your head and act like it did not happen so you can focus on school and graduating? I did, though it was hard. I did not speak a word of it after that.

I did try to commit suicide at 17 because what kept playing over and over in my head was it was my fault it happened to me because this was what my mom said, and I believed everything that she said. She couldn't tell me anything wrong; she was God to me. I took a lot of antibiotic pills but they just made my stomach hurt really badly. I did go to the hospital for a couple of hours and they sent me back home and yup, you guessed it, I had to act like that didn't happen either and I didn't get any type of counseling or therapy for my rape or attempted suicide.

Right before I graduated from high school my mother came to me and said, "I'm going to let you have your last two checks." At this point I was clueless as to what checks she was talking about. She said, "I've been getting checks for you and they are about to cut you off" because I was turning 19 two days after I graduated. I didn't question it. The checks were almost $700 dollars a month so I took those two checks and bought my first car off the car lot. It wasn't until I started my healing journey that I put two and two together and realized that all those years that I could never do anything, and she would say I was slow and me being held back in kindergarten were all for a check. I suffered all those years for a check. Just to know that haunted me. The abuse did not stop; it became more mental and emotional abuse, and the crazy part about it all is that I loved my mother even harder and deeper.

There was not a transition conversation about entering into womanhood at all. The only thing that was important to her was I looked good, and I was to make her look good—fuck how I felt. As long as the outer appearance looked good, that was what mattered to her most. Well eventually, I had my first child and moved out, and of course, she wanted to control my parenting, run my house—just my life in general. I did everything in my power to get or even feel her love back for me, but I got nothing my expectation for my mother was not my vision of her. My mother is a strong black woman just like our culture says she should be, but her being so strong broke me in two. In addition, knowing now that her being so strong was hiding some deep hurt, but me not knowing that was not my hurt or pain to carry, I took on all her baggage and then some. In addition, what I found is that your children will repeat what you do not heal. Moreover, that is where generational curses come from. I never was encouraged or received a loving word from her. I have never heard the words "I love you" escape her lips. I felt worthless to the one person that was supposed to love me forever, my own mother, and I could not stand it any longer.

So, I started to slowly disconnect from her and stand my ground with her. She didn't like that at all, so she spread this nasty rumor out that my daughter was molested and that was not true at all.

That was one of her tactics to gain control of me again, by trying to take my daughter away. In addition, like any momma bear protecting her cub I went in headfirst to protect my only child against her. Well, that situation triggered my rape memories and I had never felt so low in over 19 years. I had never felt those emotions at all because I had to act as if my rape did not happen and that took me to my darkest moment in my life ever. So, I went to no contact with her completely. I could not understand why she hated me so badly. I did nothing but want to live my own life. I had escaped her grip on my life, so I thought but I was not free from the thoughts of WHY ME? That lasted six years, until that day in December 2019 where I wanted it all to end: the thoughts, the guilt, shame, blame, anger, bitterness, resentment. I was tired of feeling this way every day, pretending to the world and society that I was doing just fine while drowning inside, with a fake smile from day to day because I couldn't tell anybody how my life really was. I was too ashamed and not only that, who would believe me if I told them?

Therefore, I left my home with the intent of not returning this time I was going through with suicide this time and no one was there to stop me. HOWEVER, GOD WAS… I haven't the slightest clue how I got on the mountain—I don't even remember—but I was there, screaming, "GOD, what do you want from me?" And in that moment that still voice spoke to my spirit and told me to surrender my life over to him and that he would give me everything that I needed. I remember wailing not crying. There is a difference. Trust me, if you ever hit rock bottom you know what I am talking about. I started saying, "I surrender" repeatedly and at that very moment it was as if a ton of bricks had been lifted off my life. I wiped my face as if nothing happened, put my trust in God and headed home. In addition, God has been leading my healing journey ever since. I started going to therapy to help balance out and control my emotions so that my emotions would never control my life again and learned how to deal with my triggers when I feel like I am experiencing a memory or flashback. This was the best decision that I made for myself. I have learned to love my mother from a safe distance and work on bettering my life for me and my daughter and everyone who comes after her because they deserve sanity, love, support, and encouragement. I chose to stop running from my issues and face them head-on. I am a generational curse-breaker, a survivor and a warrior all put together.

God gave me a vision to start an organization called H.O.P.E (Healing Over Paralyzed Emotions) to help pre-teens and women overcome the feeling of hopelessness, neglect and abandonment brought on by being raised by a toxic parent. In addition, I help them uncover their feelings and emotions that have kept them feeling paralyzed. I was going to take my pain to my grave, but God spoke and said, "Someone needs to hear your truth." God is bigger than your and my problems. I acknowledge that I was a victim of my mother's pain BUT I refuse to own being a victim anymore and I know that was never my pain to carry in the first place. I went from broken pieces to peace since acknowledging that. Do not sacrifice your own life another day to the pain you hold; let it go and be free. It was never your pain to carry in the first place.

Victoria was born in Los Angeles California to Mexican parents. She received her Master of Social Work from the University of Southern California (USC) and her Bachelor of Arts (B.A) in Deaf Studies from California State University Northridge (CSUN).

Currently she is a Licensed Clinical Social Worker (LCSW) in the state of California working as a therapist as part of a group private practice.

Victoria Serratos

Childhood Nightmare

Victoria Serratos

Growing up

I am a first generation Mexican American, born to parents who emigrated from Mexico to California in the 70s. I was born at USC Medical Center one month premature. I can recall my late mother saying that she stopped going to medical appointments when she was pregnant with me because doctors told her it would be wise to abort me. The chances of survival for either of us were low and of my being born with a cognitive disability high. My mother went to get a second opinion with the same results. My mother decided to leave our fate in God's hands. When I was born my mother told me she counted every finger and every toe multiple times to make sure nothing was missing. I was her miracle baby.

I was born in the city of Los Angeles but was raised in the San Fernando Valley, in the city of North Hollywood, California. I was raised with four older brothers, the oldest being 10 years older than me. My childhood up to age 12 was good, even though we lived in a low income, gang-infested neighborhood. We lived below the poverty line. Going to the park and getting free lunches, big blocks of government cheese and powdered milk was my younger life. I never went to the beach as a child even though we lived an hour away. I never learned how to swim because we would not go to public pools (Mom felt they were unsanitary), we received food stamps (when they were food stamps, paper money, not plastic EBT cards), and we also received financial government assistance. My mother was physically disabled and unable to work, so my father was the sole provider. My mother was in and out of hospitals. She suffered from kidney issues and began getting dialysis three times a week starting when I was just two years old. I have many memories of hospital visits, but one that is easy to recall is when I was six or seven; she fell into a coma for two days. I don't recall what the reason was. My mother later informed me she had fallen into a coma when I got older. At six I experienced an event that was traumatizing. It would have an effect on my interactions with the opposite sex. No little girl should ever have to experience such events. Unfortunately, it is a very common occurrence in society, but that is a story for another time.

First Loss

Everything changed on October 15, 1992. I had just turned 12 years old. One of my brother's girlfriends came to take me to the store to buy a troll doll. I don't know if any you reading this remember those dolls. They weren't like today's troll dolls, all colorful and cute looking. They were hideous-looking dolls, but I wanted one. So, my brother's girlfriend took me to the store to get a troll doll. When we returned, we were greeted by flashing lights coming from police cars and ambulances. As we walked up to the apartment building where I lived, I saw one of my friends and I asked, "What happened?" She was so serious when I approached her, I giggled a bit, not knowing the gravity of the situation. She said, "Don't laugh, go ask your mom." Before she said go ask your mom, I thought something might have happened to my mom. At this point my mom had been living with kidney issues for 10 years now. Running to our apartment and next is a bit of a blur. I walked in; my mom was on the floor on her knees crying and yelling, "They shot him, they shot him!" I said, "What?" not understanding what I was hearing. She said, "They shot your father." My father was a victim of a drive-by shooting.

There were theories that it was revenge because he had scared away a couple of gang members in the area after they tried to break into his garage with welding tools. Finding my mother on the ground, I had a blackout moment. At the hospital waiting for news, I remember seeing a doctor walking toward us to tell us, "We are very sorry. We tried everything we could, but he bled out during the ambulance ride to the hospital; we tried to resuscitate him without success." We were informed that he had been shot in the jugular on the ride side of the neck and bled out in the ambulance.

At the funeral, I remember feeling scared. I was scared to get close to the casket. The makeup they put on my father made him look like a vampire in my young mind (smooth face, no wrinkles, with rosy cheeks). I remember being able to get close by focusing on the side of his face that was not in public view, the side that did not have makeup on. I thought, *There's my Dad.*

The week following his death was a blur. I was in shock. The realization that my father had died hit me about a week after. I started crying and my mother was on the phone and saw me and said, "I have to call you back. Vicky just realized what happened." Vicky had been my nickname since birth, given to me by a nurse because she said I was too small for the name Victoria.

After my father was shot, we relocated to a better area in the neighborhood, but it came at a cost. I went from being surrounded by children and playing outdoors to an apartment building where I was the only child and had nobody to play with. Due to the lack of children in the area and nothing to do, since mom would monop-olize the television to watch her shows—mind you, we only had one television—I began reading more, going to the library, and bringing home stacks of books. I used to read book after book. That is when my love of books and learning began.

I returned to junior high school after taking a week off. Needless to say, everybody knew what happened. My father's murder was in the news; my mother had been on television asking for financial assistance for the funeral services and arrangements, since dad was the main means of financial support. It was my first year of junior high school and I was the girl whose father was shot. I remem-ber being angry and annoyed. Everyone would stare at me, but nobody would say a thing. Thinking back to the friends I had in junior high, it would not have been the same without them.

For the next few years, it was about adjusting to life without Dad. My mother chose to start Bible study with The Jehovah's Witnesses. She was not able to study with them when Dad was alive because he opposed that religion. I too started studying and got involved with them because of my mother. For five years I'd walk home from school and get home to see my mother watching her shows. My mother was my best friend. We did everything together, even going to the local Denny's to share a dessert and talk. I recall being asked out on a date with my mother chaperoning. It felt like it was her and me against the world. My brothers were busy with their lives; only one lived with us, the second oldest. Life was unevent-ful and pretty boring—in other words, life was great.

Second Loss

June 1997....

Mother was testing an experimental dialysis treatment, peritoneal dialysis, that she could do from home. It was Monday, June 23, 1997. Coming back from a school summer event, I walked in to find my mother not doing well. She said her stomach was hurting and she did not know why. Worried about her condition, medical help was my only thought. She said, "If I am still in pain when your brother gets home, I will have him take me to the hospital." When my brother arrived, we went to the hospital. The nurses took her and said they would keep her overnight for observation. I said goodbye to my mother. I kissed her and started walking out of the room when I heard my mother tell the nurse in her broken English, "That's my baby." I turned around and smiled but when I walked out and left her behind, I started crying, as if I knew something worse was coming. Little did I know those would be the last words I would ever hear my mother say.

Tuesday my brothers received a call that my mother's pressure dropped and that she had to be intubated. We went to visit her; she could not talk since she had a tube in her mouth. I remember arriving at the hospital and being happy to see my mother even though I did not like the way she looked with a tube in her mouth. They told us they found an infection in her stomach where the dialysis implant was, and they were going to operate the following day. My mother was aware, looking at us and nodding understanding when we talked to her. I remember thinking I should tell her how much I love her just in case, and I did. I told my mother in Spanish, "Mami Te Amo." That day we went home to wait.

The next day, Wednesday, June 26, after the surgery we went to visit. She was not awake; she did not wake up while we visited. We went home to wait again. I honestly wasn't too worried since she had been in and out of the hospital for most of my childhood. I thought she would be well in a few days and come home.

Thursday, June 27 at 3:00 am, I woke up to my older brother calling my name. I remember I couldn't hear anything. He said something to me, but I couldn't make out what he was saying, then it became clear: "Vicky, Mom died." It hit me like a ton of bricks, and at the same time like all sound came back on, hearing my brothers' wailing in the background. It was surreal; again I was in shock. I didn't completely believe she was gone. We went to see her at the hospital. I was upset they took out the tube and left her tongue sticking out. It was not how I wanted to see my mother. Her body was still warm. We hung out for a bit; we all kissed her on the forehead and left. That day was difficult. An influx of people from the church showed up at my apartment to give their condolences. Since I was the active Jehovah's Witness I had to greet and talk to everyone while my brothers grieved in their room. It was a nice show of support from everyone, but being 17, I didn't feel it was my place to host everyone. I just wanted to be left alone to grieve.

The funeral was set for Saturday. Looking back, from Thursday to Saturday I was in complete denial. It felt as if any minute she would walk through the door and all would go back to normal. Saturday came. We got ready and headed to the funeral home. As I walked in, someone asked, "Are you ok?" I said, "I am fine," as I giggled. I shortly realized I was not. As we walked into the funeral home, I saw the open casket. I walked up to the casket and stood there looking at how beautiful she looked as people paid their respects. People would walk up then go sit down as I stood there looking over my mother wearing a red dress I chose for her. When the service was about to start, they asked everyone to sit down, and I couldn't. I couldn't move. I stood there holding on tight to the casket, crying, not caring about the spectacle I made. I couldn't let my mother go. Prying my fingers from the casket was the hardest thing to do and I could not. My oldest brother went to get me to sit down. He pried my fingers off the casket and as he did, I felt my legs give way and he whispered in my ear, "Vicky, don't do this; be strong" and I felt myself go emotionally numb. The service, the people, I do not recall. Standing after the service was done and accepting everyone's condolences was my only recollection. The amount of people who came to her services was a testament to the kind of woman my mother was. She cared about people, she was empathetic, she was silly, wise, friendly, and loving. Everyone who met her loved her.

The next four months were the hardest I ever had to endure. My mother and I slept in the same room. Now I was by myself. I began sleeping in her bed. I would wake up, turn to see my bed and realize she was gone over and over. It was heartbreaking every time. Every morning I felt the pain of her loss. There were days I did not want to wake up. I'd see her in my dreams, and I did not want the dream to end. As an adult, I realized that I fell into a depression and nobody noticed. My mother passed the summer before my senior year began. My senior picture appointment was originally set on my mother's funeral day. Needless to say, I had to reschedule.

At this time, I still lived with my brother. He would wake up early and go to work, leaving me to wake myself up. The first few months of my senior year I arrived late daily, walking into class as first period was ending, feeling sad and angry. One day as I was a block away from school a California Highway Patrol officer stopped me to ask why I was not in school. With an attitude I said, "I am running late; can you not see I am walking toward school, not away from it?" I was failing most of my classes. I received my progress report and most all classes said in danger of failing, I recall thinking, *I can't not graduate; what would my mother say? I don't want to disappoint her.* That is one thought that has driven me to do better, be better and strive for more. That thought helped me get to where I am now.

After school, I would arrive home to an empty apartment. It was torture being all alone with my thoughts and my grief. I wanted the pain to end. Not wanting to go on living without my mother, on certain occasions, I was close to taking my own life. I began self-harming. The physical pain would help relieve the emotional pain. The cuts were also a physical representation of the emotional wounds.

Growing up in a Mexican household, we knew nothing about therapy. I am not surprised that adults around me never mentioned me going to therapy. The best idea to help came from the brother I lived with. Around November of 1997 my brother decided it would be a good idea to get a pet. I think I scared him one day when he was getting ready to go out in a date. I fainted; I was not eating much. My brother and I went halves on a little Chihuahua that we got from the PennySaver. I named her Onyx because she was a little black dog. I chose Onyx out of both dogs that were brought because she appeared to be calmer. Since early childhood, I had a fear of dogs. I don't know where it stemmed from, but Onyx helped me in many ways. Little Onyx gave me a reason for living and helped me get rid of my fear of dogs.

Needless to say, my parents' deaths made an impact in my life in many ways. The last year of high school I graduated by the grace of God. Some of my teachers passed me out of pity because I was close to failing their classes, most tests, and most assignments. I was too depressed, and it was too difficult to make myself care. I didn't attend college right after high school. I didn't feel like it was for me. Going to cosmetology school was more appealing. After a year, I graduated but I didn't start working in that field for a while. I wasn't confident about my ability. I continued to work as a server at restaurants in Universal Citywalk. Many things happened in my personal life at this time. I got married at 19. It was a mistake but like the saying says, "Hindsight is 20/20." I got married for multiple reasons, even though looking back, none of the reasons were a good enough excuse, but I was young and dumb. One reason was three out of four brothers were getting married around that time and I felt I was going to be left on my own. Second, as a Jehovah's Witness you date to marry, so my boyfriend at that time asked and I said yes. The marriage lasted less than a year and it was annulled, and I was excommunicated from the religion. At age 21, I left the Jehovah's Witnesses.

I lived alone from the ages of 21 to 24, until my youngest brother and I found an apartment together to help each other financially. At 21 I started dating an older married man. He told me he wasn't happy, and he was going to leave his wife. I stayed with him a year and realized he was a sore loser after a jealous rage he had where he burned a plastic doll he gave me. There was lots of smoke and it triggered the alarm. Police and firemen arrived, and he was taken to jail on arson charges. As I jumped from relationship to relationship, it was rare if I took more than a month to myself before I was in a relationship or dated again, looking for love and affection but confusing love with lust. I had to learn the hard way that some people do not love you, they lust for you and that is not the same.

I was angry for many years because I could not understand why my parents had to die when I was a child. It felt very unfair. I missed my father after he died but I was devastated after my mother died and to be honest, I've missed her more throughout my life. When my father died, I felt that I could live without my father because I had my mother but when my mother died, there were times that I have felt I could not go on living without her. It has been the hardest thing I have had to endure up to this day.

Around 22 I decided to go back to college, remembering how much emphasis my mother put on education. Working at a beauty salon as a hairstylist assistant on my feet all day, I remember thinking, *Do I want to do this type of work for the rest of my life?* Pushing us to get higher education, my mother would tell me to get a career and a good paying job so I wouldn't have to rely on a man for financial support. So, I enrolled in Los Angeles Valley College (LAVC) and went there for three years—three years because I went crazy taking classes that were interesting but didn't count toward the transfer. After three years I transferred to California State University Northridge (CSUN). I enrolled in their Deaf Studies school and went into the sign language interpreter program following the advice of one of my professors. I graduated four years later. I was 29 at this point.

I continued to be angry for a long time with the higher powers after my mother died. My thinking was negative, pessimistic, and non-empathetic with others. I began searching for answers around the age of 26. Disappointed with organized religion because of experiences I had with the Jehovah's Witnesses, I read various books on spirituality and what resonated with me was non-Christian spirituality. I liked the idea of worshipping Mother Earth and the elements. I read about Wicca, Buddhism, Hinduism, Eastern religions, and alternate forms of spirituality.

A year after graduating CSUN, I moved to Oregon with my partner at the time. His mother came into money and she gave him about ten thousand dollars, and we used it to move to Oregon. We lived in Hillsboro, which was about 20 minutes away from Portland. We lived there for about a year and I absolutely loved it, but I decided to come back to California to get my Master's degree. We moved back and shortly after we moved back Onyx, my little dog that gave me a purpose to live, passed away. It was hard but I had two other doggies, Chubs and Max, and they helped. I know many people don't see the death of a pet as a big loss but what that little dog did for me, I cannot thank her enough for. She helped me so much in the 13 years she was with me.

When I moved back from Oregon, I applied to three different Universities with my sister-in-law's assistance, which I am very grateful for: Cal State Los Angeles (CSLA), Cal State Northridge (CSUN) and University of Southern California (USC). I was accepted to all three universities but I chose to go to USC.

USC School of Social Work

I was surprised when USC accepted me. I never imagined I would go to a prestigious school. My graduate experience was a great experience. I went into the Master's of Social Work program without really knowing what social workers do. I took a leap of faith.

The social work program at USC was intense. It honestly felt like the program was designed to break you down and then put you back together better. After the trauma that transpired in my life, I went in sympathetic but not empathetic. I would hear people's hardships and think, That sucks but that's life, gotta suck it up. The program helped me heal in more than one way. It also helped me realize that the person I was dating had an undiagnosed mental illness. I remember people at school saying if you're in a relationship this program will make you or break you. A year into my graduate program he and I broke up after six years of being together. He was exhibiting bipolar symptoms. He became obsessive and eventually verbally, mentally, and emotionally abusive. He wouldn't get help and his behavior was threatening my schooling and my future career. He would keep me up until 3 am arguing and I had to be up to go to class at 5 am. I was living off energy drinks and coffee. Close to failing out of graduate school, I'd had enough. I couldn't allow that to happen. I ended the relationship. I realized it was toxic and he was not the one for me. Three months after we broke up, I moved out and found an apartment with my younger brother again. I had to wait three months to move out because I couldn't afford to until I received my student loan. After that relationship, I dated again and unfortunately, that led to a couple more events that were traumatizing. I trusted men I shouldn't have and well, you can imagine. Like I said before, that's a story for another day.

After USC

As I got older, I began to feel that there was a reason for my existence. There was a reason my mother did not abort me and there was a reason I did not take my own life when I had the chance. Searching for "my calling," in the USC Master of Social Work program I found it. After two years of intense studies, I graduated with my Masters of Social Work. During my graduate studies I began to heal from my past losses. I was able to process my grief and make peace for a lot of it. I began to see that the negative experiences I had were all for a reason. If I never experienced negative events,

I would not be able to relate to people who are going through hardships. My perspective changed and I saw how and what I went through was difficult but part of the process for my soul's evolution.

I'm coming to realize that I haven't gone through losses, multiple traumas, and hardships to live a selfish life. My life is not for me. I am here for the service of others. Since I started working at 18, I remember feeling like I had to help others. Every employment I've had has been helping other people in one way or another.

Now in my 40s, I realize I was able to overcome the losses and the traumas in life with God's help and with help from my mother. Throughout my life, what has kept me going has been remembering my mother's sayings, phrases she got from my grandfather. When I was in my early 20s and struggling to pay rent and bills, and other times when stress would want to get the best of me, what helped me not stress too much was a saying she would mention regularly. Loosely translated from Spanish it says, "If your problem has a solution why are you worrying and if it doesn't what are you gaining by worrying?" I repeat her sayings regularly throughout my life, like mantras and they helped me get through some tough times.

At this point in my life, I am happy. I am the happiest I have been in a long time. I have an intelligent, sweet, and caring pre-teen stepdaughter, along with a rambunctious, caring, silly little two-year-old girl who loves to wreak havoc… yet still brings me unbridled joy daily. I am a Licensed Clinical Social Worker working with a group private practice, getting paid well, conducting tele-therapy, helping people who suffer from anxiety, depression, trauma, and other mental health conditions. Working from home, setting my own schedule, I have more control over my life. Having almost 41 years on this earth, I lost two very crucial people in my life. I went through hardships and traumas, but I survived and am now helping others do the same. If a little girl from an impoverished low-income neighborhood can lose her parents as a child, go through multiple traumatic events, and still graduate from a prestigious university with a Master's degree and live a great life, anyone can do it.

Anedra R. Eatman brings a unique and professional background to the business field. Prior to her human resources focus, she worked in higher and K-12 education, retail sales, and health care administration organizations. Education has played an important role in her life, which is why she successfully obtained her Master of Science degree in Management.

Anedra has always had a passion to serve people. She serves as an active board member to several local organizations within the Grand Rapids community. When you ask Anedra, what keeps her going, It's her love for her family and faith. They keep her focused, healthy and motivated to continue on her journey of purpose.

Anedra's next chapter is focused on affirming, empowering and inspiring women to live better in their purpose, the purpose that God has designed for their lives. Each woman has a special crown, uniquely designed and created only for them-Crowns up.

Better not Bitter

Anedra R. Eatman

I could hear the frustration in her voice, but it was the pain in her eyes that struck me to my core. This was not how it was supposed to be or how I ever imagined my life for me, for her, for us. This hurt, but it was just the beginning of the unintentional, yet intentional pain I would cause to my princesses, my babies. As I stood quietly, looking at her with a spaced face, she proceeded to say to me, "Just go, you're not happy and you not being happy here, with us, in this house will make us miserable, so please just go." So, I left.

Listen, leaving was one of the most selfish and yet unselfish decisions I had to make. See, to understand that context means I have to share the how—the process, that is. Before I continue with the story, allow me to share my first reflective word: *process | prä,ses, 'prō,ses| a series of actions or steps taken in order to achieve a particular end* (New Oxford American Dictionary). Many times we find ourselves making hasty decisions based on those around us, those who influence us the most. This was true for me. I had influential people around me that I trusted to provide me with insight and healthy direction, and I had an expectation that they would do so with love and care. But this was not the case. The truth is, I was influenced by manipulating, controlling, and demanding humans who did not treat me and my vulnerable spirit with care.

When I reflect on how I even got to that point of my life, it takes me all the way back to my days growing up in church. Growing up in the church and being surrounded by saints does not make you a saint nor spiritually sound. I chuckle at the fact that even as a twelve-year-old, accepting Christ in her life for the first time, going through baptismal classes and then getting baptized, I had no idea what accepting Christ into my life meant. I would learn later in life that accepting Christ was just one part of the process; getting to know him, having a relationship would be the key to my growth.

Like many young girls, I trusted humans early on in my life. I never questioned motives or even really understood what that meant. As a result, as I grew up and into my teenage years, that trust remained. It started to change as I began to experience love, sex and what's next. It was interesting how love was being shown to me. While I had a nurturing mother who loved me dearly; her raising my brothers and me as a single mom would give me the strength I needed later in life to push through and remind myself of what I had come from. But it was the lack of a father during the crucial and most influential part of my life that produced confusion for my perception of what love from a man should be or have potential to become. While this chapter is not about my daddy-girl issues, I cannot skip over the fact that I had them (see reflective word process). Acknowledging what I lacked would take me farther along than I could ever imagine. Thankfully, I had a protective older brother and special uncle in my life to provide some form of guidance and direction. This is where that selfish and intentional word pops back up from the beginning, when I shared that I would have to make decisions that would be life-changing. Had I had my father in my life the way I have him in it today, I know things would have been different. But no take-backs; everything that we go through is truly for a purpose.

As I reflect upon the word sex and how it played a part in my life, I learned that not dealing with my daddy-girl issues allowed me to detach emotionally from a man. That meant I would go through a phase of my life where I would explore myself more than I probably should have, but hey, one cannot undo want was done, but learn from it and share some life lessons (hence you are reading this chapter). Exploring myself cost me. I repeat, IT COST ME! Unhealthy relationships, friendships, and possibilities—I journeyed and found myself feeling hopeless and empty. It was not until my firstborn came into my life that I grew up. She would push me to step out of my comfort zone and deal with the emotions that my grandmother did not want to deal with her children, which trickled down to my mother. My firstborn would shake and test the foundation of what I thought was solid. She would be the first one to speak to through me, impacting more so with her silence in her early years. You see, she was one of the princesses, the older of the two, asking me to leave. I birthed this human, nurtured her, took chances on the two of us, making sacrifices that I did not know existed, and yet, here she was pleading with me to leave. Her voice was shaking, her eyes filled with tears but her compassion and love for me was present. It took just that, courage to speak up and ask the woman that she has given her counsel, her mother and friend, to leave a house that was once upon a time her home.

In that moment, the choice was mine. Oh, how it would have been easier to stay, more so for my princesses, but also for financial stability reasons, it made sense. I could simply fake it to make it, hope and pray that eventually my desire to keep my family together would keep me motivated. I wanted so badly to honor my vows and apply many teachings from influencers to my decision, but as I stared back into those 17-year-old eyes, I could not lie to her, myself, and my loved ones; it was time to leave. I referenced the word influence earlier because humans do influence our decisions. *Influence | inflooans|: the capacity to have an effect on the character, development, or behavior of someone or something, or the effect itself* (New Oxford American Dictionary).

Whether we want to admit it, like it or even agree with it, it is compelling. I have dedicated my attention to the why rather than the who. Longevity played a major role in the influence of my relationship with pastoral leadership. I would find myself going to them first, before praying or seeking Abba Father's face. I would later learn that being too close to leaders with certain titles can become a hindrance. Whether intentional or unintentional, to see you for who you are transforming into could position the relationship to be one-sided. A message that comes to mind that a ministry leader spoke on was related to being in the field and how you are in the field with people you may know, but when you come out of the field, transformed, those who remained in the field and sometimes the few that came out and knew you were there, at one point, would remind you that you were there or only see you as a field person. This is how I believed that particular pastoral team had viewed me. I had made some mistakes in my marriage, admittedly stepped out for reasons I felt were justifiable. We both went into comfortable shells and just lived. As much as I wanted to do the right thing, I was in a dark place. I was in a valley, had my tent, backpack and a sleeping bag but for some odd reason, could not pitch the tent. I rolled out the sleeping bag and chilled in the valley for a little while, but knowing I could see the mountain, had desires to even touch it, gave me some form of motivation. I have a dear friend who preached me out of my stupor. I forgave myself for everything that came to mind, gathered my things, and began to mentally walk. It would be a conversation that I had with ministry leaders that would change my perspective and my interactions with leadership going forward. Respect was always there, but how and when I go about sharing or even seeking counsel would change. In that conversation I was literally told that if I made the choice to divorce, I would bring a curse upon myself and family. Additionally, I would carry the burden of the divorce and other young couples that had been looking up to me and my marriage would want to follow my lead. Therefore, my view and how I saw them would never be the same. I actually felt condemned and reprimanded. I listened and then I respectfully responded with my stance and how I planned to move forward. From that day onward, the unhealthy attachment of influence was cut. The chain was broken.

Once again, I was mentally walking, detaching, leaving behind what was not for me, no longer allowing humans to guilt or convince me to remain in a marriage or dictate how my story would end. In fact, it took courage to speak up and push back to protect myself, but it wore me out. Mentally and spiritually I had been hit hard, and it hurt. I trusted these humans as I did in my teenage years, never questioning motives, trusting best intentions were always at the forefront. In one instance, I was antagonized for stating I would seek Abba Father's guidance before agreeing to lead or participate in ministry. I was mocked and even chastised in front of my covering, who said nothing in the moment, but later apologized for not protecting me. I did not realize until later the triggering effects those behaviors would cause when years later I would get back in ministry and serve. As I stated earlier, I expected to be treated with care. Sadly, they only saw me for who I once was, referencing the context of that former field person who no longer was in the field, but yet was continually reminded of where I came from.

It would have been considerate to have a seasoned (20-plus years of marriage) couple to share with, even receive counsel from. It would have been helpful to hear them provide insight and even speak up and out about what life experiences had taught them on their journey of longevity. I reflect back on that now and believe that this is something that churches as a whole should consider: a couples connected program so the weight to know everything is not on the shoulders of the pastoral team, but the church community. When we think about community, it should start internally. One would believe it would have been easier for me to deal with my marital issues, but it was not. On the contrary, the remnants of influence remained and turned into fear. Instead of faith guiding my decisions, I was fearful of the outcome based on that life-changing conversation. So, I remained married, partially fearful of the curse and partially simply not ready to start the process. Of course, I should have commenced with prayer, but at this phase, it felt comfortable to let it sit. Remember I mentioned the acknowledgment of an issue, which typically causes you to address it. I was not ready to address and pull the layers back. Shelving the uncertainties and unknowns was convenient and comfortable. So, I did just that. It would take another purposeful encounter for me to discover myself. Until then, I would continue to live, be fruitful and multiply, welcoming my youngest princess.

Physically leaving was harder than I ever imagined. It was sucking the life out of me. How could I, the sensible, positive Patty, always there for everyone else, let it get this far? I wanted to scream, fight, and throw in the towel, but I could not. I had to face this lurking issue that was causing anxiety. To crack open the process jar and allow the influential words of others to stick to me was why I had made a conscious choice to shelf the dysfunction. I consciously made a choice to end the dysfunction at what should have been a scenic and embracing vacation. That decision would set the trajectory of rediscovery. *Rediscovery|,rēdə'skəv(ə)rē|: the action or process of discovering again something that was forgotten or ignored* (New Oxford American Dictionary). I will not provide details on this particular vacation because honestly, the details do not matter.

Again, I am choosing to focus on what caused me to mentally check out. Triggers. That word is real, and it can cause the best of us to snap. I had a triggering moment that took me to specific moments, times, and scenarios that I did not even think I remembered. I had buried a lot of situations just to cope. If I take it back, it would go as far as me asking a man to marry me. Again, keeping this high level on the day I left, I reflect that during that time of dating, I still had not dealt with my daddy-girl issues. Chiiiillleeee, when I say we have got to do better as women and deal with our issues, it should be a requirement when a father is absent. Mercy, we have simply got to do better as a community. So having that triggering moment caused me to tap out. Literally, I tapped a button in the air. Typically, I would have retreated, talked myself out of my head, but this time, I saw the writing on the wall in blue spray paint and I literally said aloud, "Enough is enough." I screamed, yelled, fought in my shower time, and then wept. It was during the weeping that I owned my actions and decisions. Not seeking Abba Father's face on so many decisions had gotten me where I was. Not specifically referencing the trigger moment, but overall, I had allowed influencers to make me feel obligated to marry because of their religious beliefs and how they had believed it would impact my eldest princess. You know that scripture "it is better to marry than burn in sin"- paraphrasing (me, rolling my eyes). This chapter may have never made it to this book—from me, that is. No take-backs. I am laughing as I type that because I wish you could hear me say it. I say it quickly and with a smile, because all that I have gone through has truly shaped me into the woman I am today.

Many times, as we go through storms and deal with life circumstances, it can make us bitter, causing us to look at life from a victim lens. I call it the blame game. Let me blame my daddy for not being in my life. Or let me put it on my momma for her and my dad not staying together. Or let me blame it on a childhood molestation that took me 30 years to speak out on. I am just talking about me right now. But I could not and would not become a victim of the blame game. I made life decisions, whether they be right or wrong, and I am unapologetic for my decisions. The journey of rediscovery permitted me to find myself in ways I did not know existed. I speak my truths and when I hear my voice, I know who and whose I am. So, when I walked out those doors on that warm fall day, I knew that our lives would never be the same. When I got into my car and drove off, I pulled over on the side of the road and wept. When I arrived at my temporary destination, I went into my room, looked around and came to grips that it was really happening. I was choosing to do better for myself and my princesses. That day would set the motions of me making healthier choices, even when they were unpopular and made many uncomfortable. I no longer sought out permission to do what was best, I respectfully informed you. Some may be wondering why now, why speak on this life journey? I was led to do so. Your girl has been listening to Abba Father and his leading.

I had been writing a book for about ten years now. But it was never the right time. I have always been one to write and journal my thoughts and events. I would look forward to writing my thoughts because it was a way for me to state my truths, but many times, I did not always have the courage to speak on them, afraid of human opinions or even rejection (another book or chapter for this one here). I knew the opportunity would find me. I was not chasing or looking for it but would be ready for the opportunity when it was time. So, while scrolling through my social media page, my dear friend—the project author—had a social media post about a book project for women who have experienced life-changing events. I smiled and posted "that would be me." At this point in my life, I understand the importance of sharing your story when being led to do so. I am not embarrassed or looking to throw anyone under the bus or call any particular human out. I learned that owning my truths, having a vision and goals will be the source of my loss of relationships. I believe it was the late and great Dr. Myles Munroe who made the statement "vision chooses your friends. It decides where you want to go in life, it decides your company". With that, I keep the vision that Abba Father has for me close and create my goals on his leading.

I am beyond grateful for this opportunity to share a snippet of my journey. I made a choice to look at my situation to better me and not turn bitter. This chapter is dedicated to: first and foremost, my Abba Father, my protector, my provider, my gatekeeper, and my reason for choosing to be better. To my immediate family— the Eatman (Eatmon) and Bates Tribe (parents and siblings)—my cheerleaders, my counsel, and my support, thank you.

My princesses reminded me that being unhealthy for me would impact them, pushing me to see that it was okay to not be okay and ask for help and get counseling. We all needed it and because of that, we are all doing better. To my supportive tribe, prayer partners, best friends, cousin-sister, confidant, and special mentor, I am forever grateful. Each of you extended not only yourselves, but your families to the girls and me. Thank you for displaying what a village really looks like. To my supportive partner who told me from day one that our friendship would be forever, thank you for not only showing me I am deserving of more, but treating me with love and care. Last but not least, to my spiritual parents who have been a positive and healthy influence in my life, Bishop T. D., and Lady Serita Jakes—their teachings, programs and consistent outreach have been a rich blessing. Not only do I feel better equipped, but also supported, even from afar. Thank you for being who you are; it matters.

To the person reading this chapter, thank you for reading it. My prayer and hope are that you walk away knowing you are not alone. Take the three steps that I have provided—process, influence and rediscovery—and use those words as tools to guide you in finding yourself. Each of us have a purpose on this earth. Will you choose to be better or bitter? The choice is yours.

Love and Light.

About The Visionary Author

Master Coach, Blogger, Author, Speaker, Trainer and #CEOMomma, Tamara C. Gooch is the Founder and CEO of Pink Pearl, LLC, a transformational movement that magnifies the triumphant voices and stories of women with boldness, confidence, and truth.

With PheMOMenon At Forty blog & The Savvy Entrepreneurs Incubator group, a think-tank, next-level innovative learning platform, Tamara has established the concept of online community building and engagement, building and creating an elite, high-result society of everyday women who are impacting the world in monumental ways. Her formula for success is simple – Faith, Fierceness, Fearlessness, Fabulousness, Action, and incessant Education.

Tamara propels her clients forward with the blueprint and tools needed to launch and grow a successful business and monetize their genius in the most efficient way, while enjoying their lives, time with family, and a lifestyle of freedom.

Tamara C. Gooch

www.ingramcontent.com/pod-product-compliance
Lightning Source LLC
Chambersburg PA
CBHW052102270326
41931CB00012B/2859